CREATING YOUR LIFE

A Lifetime of Learning, Book 1

Mark Andre Alexander

Make clear distinctions,
and examine all things well.
The Golden Verses of
Pythagoras

THE SCHOOL OF
PYTHAGORAS™
Auburn, CA

MarkAndreAlexander.com
/Iamresearch/
Password: Lam1

Published by Mark Andre Alexander
P.O. Box 5286, Auburn, CA 95604-5286

Third Edition

Library of Congress Cataloging-in-Publication Data

Alexander, Mark Andre, 1956-
Creating your life: a lifetime of learning / by Mark Andre
Alexander

p. cm. — (A Lifetime of Learning, Book 1)
ISBN 978-1-937597-20-7

Cover design by Melinda De Ross: www.coveredbymelinda.com

Photos and illustrations are created by the author, in the public
domain, or licensed from Thinkstock.com™, PhotoDisc®, and
Nova Development Corporation.

Version 4_0

Thanks to my readers: Bree, Scott, and Christine. Also, thanks to
BubbleCow.Com for great editing services at reasonable prices.

Go to MarkAndreAlexander.Com to access a free 36-day course
on *Creating Your Life.*

Subscribe to the "Creating Your Life" channel on YouTube.

Also by Mark Andre Alexander

Money and Wealth: A Lifetime of Learning, Book 2
Sex and Romance: A Lifetime of Learning, Book 3
Mozart and Great Music: A Lifetime of Learning, Book 4

Handbook for Advanced Souls: Eternal Reminders for the Present Moment

Public domain works edited by Mark Andre Alexander

Hamlet and the Scottish Succession by Lilian Winstanley
Shakespeare's Law and Latin by Sir George Greenwood, M.P.
The George Greenwood Collection

CONTENTS

For Bree and HK,
and those who Quest

About This Series

How many times have we said it to ourselves? *If I only knew then what I know now?*

This series of little books, titled *A Lifetime of Learning*, gives my personal, and admittedly idiosyncratic, discoveries over the years. I wish I had these gems in my teens. Discoveries, I now find, most adults still seem to have missed.

Of course, I may not have acted on that knowledge, but still it would have been nice to know.

In many cases, knowing then what I know now would have saved me time, money, and heartache; would have enriched me, and given me greater personal freedom.

This first book, on *Creating Your Life*, extracts what I have learned about setting goals, both personally and professionally. Part is based on a project I delivered for my Master's degree in Organization and Management Development.

I start the series with this book because the ideas expressed here form a foundation for the rest of the series.

How does our life get created? How does our mind limit us? What is Truth?

The publishing imprint I have chosen, The School of Pythagoras, points to the quest for the fundamental nature of Truth.

This series is dedicated to those of you on that quest.

Introduction

*I am enough of an artist
to draw freely upon my imagination.
Imagination is more important than knowledge.
Knowledge is limited.
Imagination encircles the world.*
Albert Einstein

If you learn one thing only from this little book, then let it be this:

**Imagination is the tool
with which you architect your life,
and if you don't use it, others surely will.**

In simple language, *use* your imagination, your ability to picture, to daydream, to play in your mind's eye. Why? Because imagination is the engine of your life.

Look around you. Look at your home, the furniture, the walls, your clothes, your computer, your TV, and videogames. Look outside at the lawn, the sidewalk, the cars, the trucks, the bicycles, the toys, the roads, and almost all you can see.

Everything started in someone's imagination.

Someone imagined the chair you're sitting in, the guitar sitting in the corner, the arch of the ceiling.

Someone imagined creating the silicon chip that went into someone's imagining your smartphone and someone else's imagining the software that runs it all to create something amazing.

Imagination is the tool that you must begin using in a more advanced way if you want to take charge of and create your life.

Do not think creating your life is easy. That it just *happens* if you imagine it and do nothing. For most people, it's hard work.

There is an entertaining notion in Malcolm Gladwell's book *Outliers: The Story of Success*. He says it takes 10,000 hours of effort to master something. He talks about The Beatles, a 1960s rock group who performed live in Germany, eight hours in a day, over 1,200 times between 1960 and 1964. They put in 10,000 hours of performing and achieved incredible success.

Mozart's father started teaching him music at the age of three. Mozart put in so much time practicing and composing that he achieved 10,000 hours by age 14.

Bill Gates had completed 10,000 hours of computer programming by the time he started Microsoft.

So what do you want to create?
What kind of life do you want to lead?
What do you love so much that you would spend 10,000 hours mastering it, and then making money doing what you love?

You may not want to be Mozart or Bill Gates. You may not want to be a master of one thing. Perhaps you want to be excellent at several things, putting in 3,000 or 5,000 hours into each.

Or maybe you want to be just really good at a number of things and put 1,000 or 2,000 hours into them: playing the guitar, rebuilding an engine, snow skiing, cooking a romantic meal.

In his novel *Time Enough for Love,* through the character Lazarus Long, Robert Heinlein wrote:

> A human being should be able to change a diaper, plan an invasion, butcher a hog, conn a ship, design a building, write a sonnet, balance accounts, build a wall, set a bone, comfort the dying, take orders, give orders, cooperate, act alone, solve equations, analyze a new problem, pitch manure, program a computer, cook a tasty meal, fight efficiently, die gallantly. Specialization is for insects.

Perhaps...

Mozart and Bill Gates were master specialists, and the world fascinates us more because they were.

But master generalists are important as well.

So how will you create your life?

Will you be a generalist or a specialist?

What do you need to know to increase your ability to take charge of your future?

How This Little Book Can Help

Your mind has the ability to inhibit or enhance your imagination. This book shows you secrets of how your mind works. It gives you keys to being a success by simply thinking differently and acting in new ways.

There are no guarantees. You may not always get exactly what you imagine. The world simply doesn't work that way.

But if you learn and apply what this little book shows you, you will move more quickly into becoming the person you have always wanted to be.

> You can carry images and emotions like a bag full of rocks that weigh you down and interfere with your goals.

> Letting go of the rocks not only gives you room to breathe, but also creates space for incredible creative energy.

Now for a glimpse into what follows:

Chapter 1: What Is Imagination? explores the mystery of your creative power.

Chapter 2: Blind Spots shows you how your mind can blind you to the truth.

Chapter 3: The Reticular Activating System discloses a powerful part of your mind that shapes every moment of every day.

Chapter 4: Your Reality Thermostat explains how your pictures of yourself and the world can be enhanced or restricted.

Chapter 5: The Subconscious Repository reveals how the subconscious mind works to limit and support your goals.

Chapter 6: The Adaptive Unconscious shows you how there is a part of your mind that constantly and secretly shapes your world.

Chapter 7: Picture Power talks about experts and how they can actually limit you.

Chapter 8: Self-Talk and Self-Image delves deeply into how you create yourself and your world.

Chapter 9: Affirmations provides you examples of how to work with the mechanisms of your mind with imagination exercises to manifest your life.

Chapter 10: Opening Windows of Opportunity suggests actions that will make you move quickly toward your goals.

Chapter 11: Advanced Imagination: Creating from Soul offers you an out-of-the-box way of creating your life without using your mind.

Chapter 12: Next Steps suggests how to bring more adventure into creating your life.

Next you will find a *Creating Your Life* checklist and a recommended reading list, as well as an appendix that offers details for the more scholarly readers.

The keys in this book, faithfully applied, *do* deliver results. You have to experience the results yourself to realize fully the value of this new kind of imaginative thinking and goal setting.

So let's begin this marvelous adventure.

Chapter 1

What Is Imagination?

When patterns are broken, new worlds emerge.
Tuli Kupferberg, poet

Philosophers like to distinguish *memory* from *imagination*.

We perceive sounds, smells, tastes, and experiences. We can close our eyes and recall these same sounds, smells, tastes, and experiences. We can remember what we ate yesterday, how we felt the first time we kissed someone, what bioluminescent ocean waves look and sound like. (Search YouTube.com to see such waves.)

We call this faculty of the mind "memory."
We remember the past.

What about the future?

We know we can take past experiences and change them to picture something we haven't experienced. I can have memories of touching a hot stove, blistering my finger, and also watching a campfire burn.

However, I can *imagine* putting my hand in a campfire and *feeling and seeing* my hand burn. It does not matter that I have never experienced actually putting my hand in a campfire. I can picture it. I can imagine it.

We call this faculty of the mind "imagination."
We can picture what is not real.
Or what we have not yet experienced.

We can imagine bioluminescent ocean waves that are green or yellow, or waves with images of colorful birds in them. We can imagine the ocean waves falling up in curious spirals with the sounds of trumpets and flutes coming out of the shooting spray, and the smell of peaches in the spray.

Even though we have never seen
or heard such things combined.

So imagination is not limited to images or mere memory. All senses can be put into play. And make no mistake, imagination is *play*. Daydreaming is playful. And the more we know how our mind works, the more we can take advantage of playful daydreaming.

What happens when a girl first sees someone dance on stage and begins imagining that *she* is the dancer? How is it that creative drive provides the energy for the girl to beg her parents for dance lessons, and in a few years she is dancing onstage herself?

What happens when a boy sees firefighters in a fire truck and begins imagining that *he* is a firefighter? How is it that creative drive provides the energy for the boy to read all about firefighters, to discover what he needs to be a firefighter, and then someday to find himself bravely running into burning buildings?

How is it that some people build a multimillion dollar business, and when that business fails, they sink into depression? Yet others who fail building a multimillion dollar business turn around and build another one, and another?

Once you have an understanding of how the mind works, and how imagination creates your world, you will have the keys to create and change your life.

First, let's look at the nature of mental blind spots. Then we can explore how and why your mind creates them, for better or worse.

Chapter 2

Blind Spots

We think and act not in accordance with
the real truth, but the truth as we believe it.
Lou Tice, coach

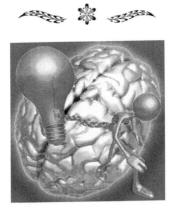

Is seeing believing?

Take a moment and read what's in the triangle on the next page:

It says, "PARIS IN THE SPRING," right?

Wrong. Read it again.

Isn't it interesting how easily our mind creates a blind spot to what's actually there? You see the two THEs, right?

But maybe you've already seen this Paris Triangle before. Try this sentence:

> FINISHED FILES ARE THE RESULT
> OF YEARS OF SCIENTIFIC STUDY
> COMBINED WITH THE EXPERIENCE
> OF MANY YEARS OF EXPERTS.

Now go back and read the sentence one time and count the letters "F." How many "Fs" are there? STOP! Do not read on until you have counted the "Fs" in the sentence.

Most people find three "Fs." However, there are seven "Fs." Go back and find them.

Still not seeing them? About 50% of people who read this sentence see only three "Fs" even after being told there are more. Isn't it strange? You can be told that there are seven "Fs" and yet you *still* can't see them.

If you don't believe me, go back and count the "OFs" in the sentence.

Watch this Psychological Card Trick on YouTube.

http://www.youtube.com/watch?v=mvzSiUB6yV0

How does he do it? Watch it again and you may figure it out.

Watch the following Cards Awareness Test #1 on YouTube, which has you count the number of red suit cards.

http://www.youtube.com/watch?v=-7Ec6tTwkqg

Did you see the secret message? Isn't it interesting how easily we can be blind to something happening right in front of us when we focus on something else nearby? (This is one secret of magicians and con artists.)

The same is true with this Passing the Basketball video.

http://www.youtube.com/watch?v=IGQmdoK_ZfY

For those of you already familiar with this illusion, did you spot the two additional changes that took place right in front of your eyes?

Okay. So what? A few optical illusions, right? No big deal.

Well, it *is* a big deal, especially if you are concerned about seeing *Truth* in the world and inside of yourself.

It is a big deal if you go around
unaware that you have blind spots
to the Truth.

Great high-performing people, in sports or business or anywhere else, demonstrate an ability to focus and block out distractions, to create blind spots to everything irrelevant to what they are focusing on.

The basketball video demonstrates that when you *focus* on something, you may become *blind* to everything else. This ability to focus is good up to a point.

But there is a down side as well. When you lock on to what you believe the truth to be (or the "purpose" to be, like the purpose given to you to count the number of passes between players in white) that missile-lock can blind you to other important things going on.

This is how magicians work. And it's how advertisers, media manipulators, politicians, and con artists generally work. They get you to lock on to one thing so you are blind to something else.

When you lock on to one "truth,"
you may be locking out the real Truth.

The fact is, if you want to change, to grow, to get to the *Truth*, whatever it may be, you may want to consider a few things:

1) How are blind spots created?

2) Do I have blind spots that limit or control me and my imagination?

3) How can I discover my blind spots?

4) How can I avoid creating blind spots that limit or control me?

5) How can I recognize blind spots in other people?

6) How can I recognize when others are intentionally or unintentionally trying to create blind spots in me?

7) How can I get past blind spots and into imagining and creating my life in a free-flowing manner with abundant energy?

> *Your blind spots may be keeping you*
> *from having spontaneous*
> *and continuing energy*
> *to accomplish your goals.*

The fact is, you are probably living only a small part of your potential. You hold these blind spots in the form of pictures about yourself, about others, and about reality. They keep you from doing what you are fully capable of doing.

Once you understand that, you can take more conscious control of creating your life.

Now let's look more closely at how the mind creates blind spots.

Chapter 3

The Reticular Activating System

*A truly creative person rids him or herself
of all self-imposed limitations.*
Gerald Jampolsky

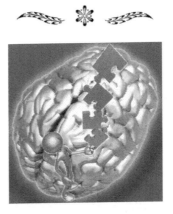

**Your mind has a powerful filtering system that creates
blind spots.**

Have you noticed how when you read a book and
the story fills your imagination, the outer world
begins to fade away? You don't hear the traffic

outside or someone calling for you. They have to speak more loudly just to get through to you.

Have you noticed how you can be at a party with everyone talking and you can hardly understand what anyone is saying? But when someone mentions your name, that gets through to you?

Have you noticed how when you fall asleep your senses slowly shut down, your body loses sensation, and then you are off to sleep? Then almost nothing gets through to you?

Our senses take in 11 million pieces of data in each moment, but we can only consciously process up to 40 pieces per second.

The part of your brain working as a filter to manage sense perception is called the Reticular Activating System (RAS).

If the mind didn't have the RAS, you'd go crazy. Think of all the information coming in through all your senses. The sights, the sounds, the tactile sensations.

Think of all those little hairs on your body. If you focus on any part of your body, you would become aware of the sensation there.

The RAS is a network of cells in the center of the brain associated with waking, sleeping, attention, and focus. It physically filters irrelevant sensory input.

The RAS allows you to focus. It functions like an executive assistant, a kind of censor of what's not important. It screens out the junk.

The RAS determines what information gets through to you.

What you Value, or what you think is a Threat.

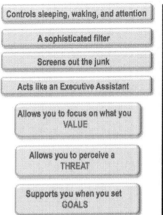

- Controls sleeping, waking, and attention
- A sophisticated filter
- Screens out the junk
- Acts like an Executive Assistant
- Allows you to focus on what you VALUE
- Allows you to perceive a THREAT
- Supports you when you set GOALS

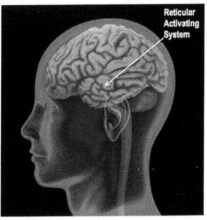

Reticular Activating System

As we focus on something important, things that are less important, things that we *Devalue*, fade away. Important information gets through, whatever we consider valuable or threatening.

This explains why teenagers can be watching TV or playing a video game, and a parent can call them to dinner and not be heard. The *Value* of the parent's voice goes down in proportion to the importance of the TV.

This explains why eight people at a large dinner table can have cross conversations with each other and still carry on. As you focus on something important like your own conversation, the others nearby fade because they lose *Value* to you.

This explains why a new mother sleeps through the alarm clock going off, the jet flying overhead, and the truck driving by, but when the baby starts crying, she wakes up right away. The other sounds are not a *Threat* so they don't get through the censor, but the threatening sound of the baby gets through.

> *What you Value gets through.*
> *What you Devalue gets filtered out.*

But the owners loved their dog and were comforted and felt protected by its barking. They would have no problem sleeping through the night. Their neighbors may also have slept better if they knew that any burglars in the area would be warned off by a barking dog.

Once I worked at a company that decided to move my group to a different building. I was placed next to a service elevator.

You can imagine what that means. All day long, every day, I would hear that elevator opening and closing, opening and closing.

What did I do?

Because I knew about the RAS, I immediately told myself, "That elevator doesn't matter to me."

When people asked me, "Isn't that elevator going to bug you all day?" I'd answer, "No, I won't even notice it."

And almost from the beginning my RAS screened it out. It never bothered me.

A colleague who used to have an office was now in an open cube. He did not know about the RAS. He was used to closing the door and having quiet.

He would hear me talking on the phone over two cubes away and he would stand up and say, "Mark, you are talking too loud."

Every sound was a threat to him, so every sound got through.

The key is knowing that *you control* what gets through.

> *It depends on how you psychologically evaluate the sensation.*

This fact is particularly important to teachers.

How often do we accuse a child of not paying attention to the teacher? But what if the teacher is not making the history lesson, or math lesson, or science lesson *interesting* to the child?

> *The teacher and the course material fade away.*

The child can be looking right at a teacher as the teacher explains something and not get it.

(We all have experienced this. We lose interest, our minds wander, the filters kick in because we become interested in our own thoughts or daydreaming. And minutes go by where nothing the teacher/boss/television/politician says gets through.)

What happens when the child sees no *Value* in what the teacher is saying?

The child's RAS screens out the teacher. It's the teacher's job to make sure the class material is perceived as valuable by the child.

So the question is, what do you *Value* in life? And what do you *Devalue*?

Because now you know that if you devalue important things, they will not get through your mind's automatic filter.

> *What do you Devalue?*
> *Could what you Devalue actually hold Value?*
> *How will you know if you are blind to it?*

Now let's look at how the mind can automatically regulate your perception of reality.

Chapter 4

Your Reality Thermostat

If you put yourself in a position where
you have to stretch outside your comfort zone,
then you are forced to expand your consciousness.
Les Brown

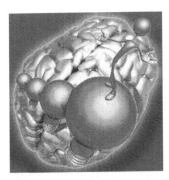

The mind contains a kind of thermostat that keeps us within "Reality."

A thermostat works to keep the temperature within a certain range.

If the temperature rises too high, the thermostat turns on the air conditioner. If the temperature sinks too low, the thermostat turns on the heater.

> For example, if we set the temperature at 70 degrees Fahrenheit, there's usually a 4-degree range from 68 to 72 that does not cause the heating or cooling to go on. This is called the Comfort Zone.
>
> But if the temperature falls below 68, the heater turns on and heats up to 70, and then shuts off.
>
> If the temperature goes above 72, the air conditioning turns on and cools it down to 70, and then shuts off.

Automatic Temperature Regulation

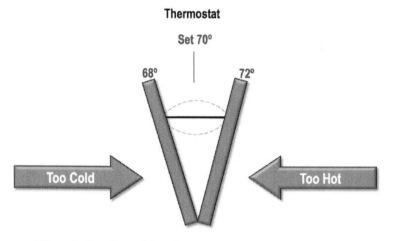

The whole idea of the thermostat is to keep the temperature within the Comfort Zone— automatically.

The mind has its own deep, innate mechanism, like a thermostat, that continually tries to make sense of the world, to keep the world within a comfortable range. Within what we think of as "Comfortable Reality."

It's part of the subconscious mind that regulates how we see the world. It holds a certain picture of the world we label Reality. It also holds a certain picture of ourselves, our Self-Image, which we label as "Who I am."

Then it goes to work making sure that everything we perceive fits in with our picture of "Who I am" in the Real World.

Automatic Behavior Regulation

Sanity Thermostat

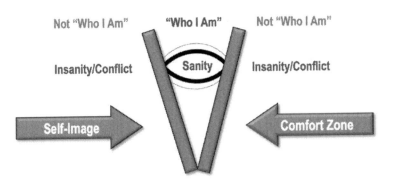

But this picture is not the same for everybody. Different people have different pictures about what is real and what is not real. They have different pictures about themselves and about the world out there. Most of us have enough of a similar picture that we can get along with each other.

But people with a picture that deviates too much from our common picture begin to look crazy to us. This fact often accounts for the strife between people with different politics or religions.

Here's an example...

Everybody tends to accept certain authorities as true authorities. We tend to believe in experts who tell us something about ourselves. In elementary school they have these tests that show us our strengths and weaknesses. Usually verbal and math, right?

> So suppose a student in elementary school takes one of these tests, and the teacher, an authority figure, tells her that she's weak in math. She takes that in. "I'm weak in math. Thanks for telling me. I might have tried."

> > *For the student, that becomes the "Truth,"*
> > *whether or not the test is accurate.*

> Her internal picture of herself sets the thermostat, "Who I am". Once that truth gets embedded, the student's mind will reaffirm that truth every time she fails a test.

> And if she does well on a test? The thermostat in her mind will see that as a mistake; therefore, she looks at it as a mistake.

> Scientific studies show that the next time she takes a test *she'll do poorly.*

> > *Her subconscious picture will help her*
> > *correct for the mistake of success.*

26

Her mental thermostat has been set to, "I'm weak in math." Being good at math does not fit her picture of herself, and anything that contradicts that picture is seen as an error, a fluke. Even success. Because success is not "Who I am."

If you are a middle-class or upper-class person, you can see what happens when you get outside your Reality comfort zone by driving into a poverty-stricken or ghetto neighborhood. Unless you're already used to helping out in such a neighborhood, you will get nervous, sweaty, and have a strong urge to get out as quickly as possible.

It's not your kind of neighborhood. It does not match the picture you have of what a neighborhood should look like.

> It's the same with some poor people who win the lottery. People picture themselves as poor, then get Big Money, only to throw it away on parties and extravagant purchases rather than investing.

> They see themselves as poor. They're comfortable with that picture because it's a picture that they are familiar with. They know the rules. Suddenly they have *Money*.

> Money puts them in an uncomfortable world. It's new, it's different. It's not like what they're used to. So they become spendthrifts and end up back in the lifestyle they are used to. They return to the comfort zone set by their internal thermostat.

> *They correct for the mistake*
> *of having too much money.*

You're probably thinking, "Well, that can't be right. There are plenty of poor people who become wealthy." Sure. But it's often through their own efforts. They hold a picture of themselves that gets them beyond their circumstances. They daydream of a different life. They get comfortable with that daydream, and then they grow into it.

And if they sustain that picture, they gradually manifest that dream.

> *They transition into*
> *the new picture of Reality.*

They have managed to reset their thermostat, take on a new picture of themselves, a new self-image, and live a different life.

Lottery winners could do that as well. It's just that many of them never see themselves with big money. They see themselves still as poor people, but with money to spend.

They could adopt a new picture of themselves and their life, and then work to create it for themselves. Because real and lasting change starts on the inside.

> *They have to do the work in resetting*
> *their own subconscious thermostat.*

Some people believe that life is merely luck. That you are what you are. That you can't change. One of the best things you can learn at a young age is that you can grow and change constantly.

You have the power to alter your thoughts,
to talk to yourself in new and positive ways;
to change your pictures.

It's time we go deeper into how the mind works so we can begin to see how to change our pictures.

Chapter 5

The Subconscious Repository

*Any thought that is passed on to the subconscious
often enough and convincingly enough
is finally accepted.*
Robert Collier

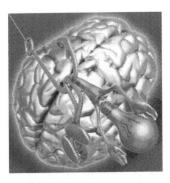

**You are bombarded every day with an endless barrage of
sensations: Sights, sounds, smells, tastes, and tactile
sensations.**

Imagine if you had to consciously sort through all that incoming data to separate the important data from the unimportant data. What sights should you notice? What sounds?

You already know that the Reticular Activating System automatically filters your perceptions. But there is more.

Your conscious mind constantly has you perform a basic series of actions as you go through the day. Each time you come upon an experience, you perceive and connect, and then you evaluate and respond with some kind of action, or no action.

> *I perceive* something running towards me and *I connect* that perception with my experience and memory—a dog, but not just any dog. A Rottweiler.

> *I evaluate* it. The last time a Rottweiler ran towards me, it bit me. This is not good. *I respond* by running away.

The Conscious Mind

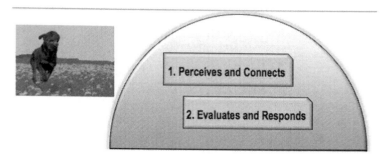

1. Perceives and Connects

2. Evaluates and Responds

We think that is pretty much all there is to reality. We assume we see everything and choose our responses. But reality is more like an iceberg. A small percentage of the whole appears above the surface.

Do you consciously go through each step? No. Somehow, your mind takes you through all these steps in milliseconds.

How does it do this so quickly? You can thank your subconscious mind.

Isn't it funny how often we hear about the fact that we have a subconscious mind, and yet we never take it into account in our daily lives? Well, it's time to start.

Because there is a significant minority of people around you who do, and sometimes they do so at your expense and their benefit.

Patterns, Habits, and Preferences

Your subconscious mind is a repository. It stores patterns, habits, and preferences. Your subconscious, especially as it relates to the RAS, constantly co-opts anything you do repeatedly and tries to make it automatic. That's its job. It responds to what you do repeatedly.

When you first start learning to drive a car, you are conscious of every turn of the wheel and movement of your feet. You have to be because it's not yet habitual.

Your subconscious notes the repetitive activity and stores the patterns. Soon, you're driving down the road for minutes at a time and you forget that you are driving.

How do you stay on the road? Your subconscious takes over and keeps you doing what you have done so many times before. It makes your driving automatic to free your conscious mind to focus on other things.

And that's it in a nutshell: The subconscious takes over whatever you do out of *habit*—whatever you repeatedly *prefer*, whatever repeated *pattern* you create—and makes it automatic.

So you don't have to think consciously.

The same is true with learning how to type. Most typing teachers will tell you that there is a 20-words-per-minute limit to conscious typing. There is a barrier that you cannot consciously pass.

When you learn how to type, you have to learn to let go, allow it to become habitual (subconscious). Then you can reach 50, 60, 100 words per minute.

Piano players and other musicians know the same thing. At first, you have to practice, practice, practice. At a certain point, proficiency and speed pick up as you allow the activity to become more automatic, more a part of your subconscious.

You don't think; you just play.

In life, we lean toward things we like and away from things we dislike. The subconscious begins to co-opt and make automatic our repeated likes and dislikes.

Our cultivated preferences become habitual. They become a part of us, and we soon believe that these preferences are instinctual, determined, and automatic, rather than learned.

The Subconscious Repository

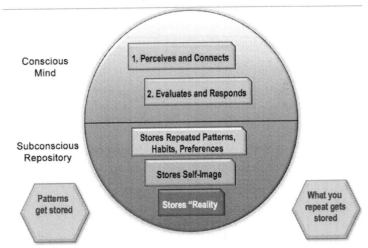

Reality

So here's the kicker—just like patterns, habits, and preferences:

> *What you repeatedly believe to be true*
> *also gets stored,*
> *whether it's true or not.*

Your subconscious is not interested in what is really true, only in what you repeatedly believe to be true.

Anything you strongly believe to be true gets stored as the "Truth," as "Reality." And it becomes part of your makeup, your personality, as integrated into you as your driving, your typing, and your preferences.

This storage includes both the "Truth" about "Reality" out there, and your picture of yourself in here. Your Self-Image.

Self-Image

What do you imagine about yourself? Is everything you imagine about yourself true?

Do you focus on the rocks in the path of your life, on what limits you?

On what actually might *not* be true about you?

Or, like when riding a bicycle, do you focus on the way around the rocks?

And we're not talking just about what you imagine. What do others imagine about you? (Your parents, friends, teachers, everyone else.) Is what they imagine about you true?

And how often do *you* imagine what *others* imagine about *you*? Do you really know?

Do you think it might be time to get some of these rocks out of your head?

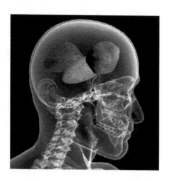

What you repeatedly imagine to be true about yourself gets stored as your *Self-Image* (your Self-Imagination).

And you are not the only one crafting it.

You hold pictures of how the world is supposed to be.

You hold pictures of how you are supposed to be.

You recall pictures from the past.

You perceive filtered pictures of the present.

You imagine pictures of the future.

To your subconscious, all pictures are Here.

Now.

In the Present.

In the book, *Soul and Spirit: A Lifetime of Learning*, we explore the implications of this fact.

For now, let's look at another mechanism of the mind that actively blinds you in interesting ways.

Chapter 6

The Adaptive Unconscious

The moment a person forms a theory, his imagination
sees in every object only the traits which favor that theory.
Thomas Jefferson

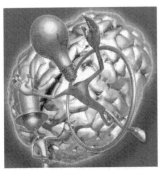

There is a part of your mind designed to regulate
automatically and unconsciously any conflicts between
"reality out there" and your stored pictures.

A third part of your mind apart from the conscious
mind and the subconscious repository, acts as a kind of

censor. One of its primary jobs is to make sense of the world. This censor keeps you balanced by making sure that "Reality" out there as you *perceive* it to be matches the "Truth" inside as you subconsciously understand it.

This censor regulates
your perception and behavior
to make sure the two pictures match.

This censor can even create blind spots to "the truth out there" in order to make sure the inner picture is not messed with. (We'll see shortly how this works.)

Recall from Chapter 5 that the conscious mind perceives and connects, evaluates and responds. The subconscious repository manages conscious thought by storing patterns, habits, and preferences. It also stores what it believes to be the truth, no matter what the real truth is.

The censor, known in cognitive science as the Adaptive Unconscious (AU), performs three primary functions:

— It aligns pictures (the inner picture and the outer).

— It maintains "Truth" or "Reality" (however you define truth or reality).

— It creates motivation (to align pictures, to maintain or change "Truth" or "Reality" as you know it, to achieve goals).

Although I talk about these three functions separately, as you will see they are really all the same.

The Adaptive Unconscious

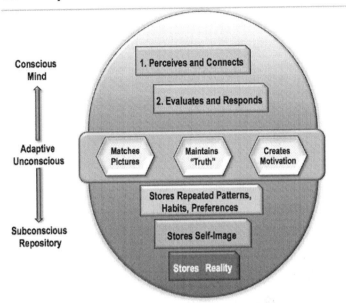

1) The AU Maintains "Truth"

The AU resolves apparent differences between inner and outer pictures. It resolves differences between the pictures you have stored in your subconscious repository and the way things appear "out there" in the world. Depending on how you hold the pictures, the differences between them can be resolved either way. Either the inner picture must change to match the outer picture, or the outer picture must change to match the inner picture.

The subconscious stores "Truth" (it is initially uncritical as to the truths that form the stored reality). Reality is stored in the form of patterns, habits, and preferences that arise as picture-patterns that we hold onto. They become our anchor points in this world.

> For example, suppose my parents told me (as they did when I was twelve) that "You can't make money doing what you love; you have to be practical."

> If I uncritically accept that picture of "Who I am," it gets stored as *true* or *reality* in my subconscious. Now immediately the AU goes to work building blind spots to anything suggesting that I actually *can* make money doing what I love.

> I begin developing patterns, habits, and preferences that reinforce the stored picture.

Why does the AU build such blind spots? Because the AU works to resolve differences between pictures, meaning anything that contradicts my *perceived* reality. The AU functions automatically and naturally. Its job is to make sense of the world. And to keep my sense of myself consistent.

As long as I believe this Reality, I cannot accept anything that contradicts it. The AU has to maintain my balance by requiring me to see only my stored Reality.

> *You can literally be*
> *looking at the opposite truth*
> *and not see it.*
> *(Remember the "Fs"?)*

Have you ever lost your smartphone, and after having looked *everywhere* you announce, "My smartphone is nowhere to be found."

Immediately, your AU builds a blind spot against you actually *seeing* the smartphone (or car keys, or purse, or whatever it is you *know* is not anywhere you looked).

Why?

Because you would appear foolish (insane) after having made your statement. Someone else finds them (in an obvious place where you had *looked* several times), and you have to say something like, "OK, who moved them? They were not here when I looked."

This phenomenon is also evident when you judge someone.

I remember working at a job where I was told that a certain fellow employee was stealing, but had yet to be caught.

I began to *see* that employee's shiftiness. Her actions were obviously suspicious. Though I had once thought her kind and ethical, now she acted in a way that reinforced her untrustworthiness.

Then the *real* culprit was caught, and suddenly she regained her kindness and innocence. The indisputable facts forced me to let go of my false inner picture of her.

2) The AU Matches Pictures

The AU helps us solve problems. In fact, once we understand the art of giving the AU our problems to solve (resolve), we can grow in remarkable ways.

> Suppose some neighbor kids break a couple of planks in my fence. The picture suddenly

doesn't match the inner picture of a well-made fence.

To resolve the conflict, my AU creates the drive for me to repair my fence and make it look "the way it should look."

But if I don't fix the fence right away, the AU will co-opt the new image of a broken fence and begin making me comfortable with the new picture. Soon, the broken fence remains broken.

The new picture gets stored. It's now a part of the Reality picture.

This fact explains why any time you have to make home repairs, it's always a good idea to do them quickly. Otherwise, the AU stores the new picture causing you to lose the motivation to change it.

The AU typically won't allow us to hold two contradictory pictures of ourselves or reality. The AU always works to resolve such cognitive dissonance because the AU makes things complete, resolves differences, solves problems.

3) The AU Creates Motivation

Suppose you set a goal to remodel your kitchen. Suddenly you have a "problem." The picture or *vision* you have does not match the *reality*. You experience cognitive dissonance and your AU moves into action to resolve the problem, to create wholeness.

You must do one of two things:

Either give up your vision
or remodel your current situation.

This form of anxiety is actually creative energy and motivation. In other words, to be creative is to deliberately create conflicting pictures between the inner and the outer (setting a goal or creating a vision) so that the AU motivates you to resolve the conflict (accomplishing the goal or vision to align with the new inner picture you are holding).

Many people avoid setting visions and goals, or accepting new interpretations, because they confuse creative energy with *stress*. To grow intellectually and professionally means to continually *revise* yourself and your picture-models of reality.

How to Quit Smoking

I used to smoke two packs of cigarettes a day.

I wanted to quit. It's hard to quit, even though research shows that the physical addiction is gone after several days of non-smoking.

Why do so many smokers go back to smoking after quitting?

Because even though they have given up smoking, they still hold the image of themselves as smokers.

*I quit smoking by
becoming a non-smoker first.*

I spent months visualizing myself without
cigarettes, even though I still smoked. I
pictured my life without smoke, without

dirty ashtrays, without a cigarette between
my fingers, even while I was smoking.

And I adopted the attitudes of a non-
smoker. Smoking is awful, it pollutes the air,
kissing smokers is like licking an ashtray.
The usual stuff.

The problem with most people who quit and
still crave cigarettes is that *they are still
smokers who aren't smoking.* The outer
picture may have changed, but they still hold
onto the subconscious picture of themselves
as smokers. And so they still crave cigarettes.

The Adaptive Unconscious tries to resolve the
conflicting pictures by creating the craving.

When I finally quit, I didn't crave cigarettes because
non-smokers don't crave cigarettes. And I was already a
non-smoker.

I worked daily to create a new inner picture, one that
ended up being so strong that the outer Reality had to
change.

What kind of person are you?

What ways do you picture yourself that hold you back from what you want to be?

There is rarely an easy way to change, and not everything will submit to your efforts.

I know this sounds simplistic. But you have nothing to lose by becoming aware of the processes involved. And trying a few experiments. You might be surprised at how you begin creating your life.

If you have the discipline
and are willing to do the work.

Now let's look closely at the power these pictures hold.

Chapter 7

Picture Power

Science is the belief in the ignorance of experts.
Richard Feynman

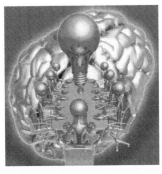

Do you trust the experts?

In Australia a 600-km marathon is held every year between the cities of Sydney and Melbourne.

Back in the 1980s, a 61-year-old man named Cliff Young showed up to run in the race. (You can read about him on Wikipedia.) All the world-class runners thought he was some homeless person who showed up in the wrong place.

Why?

Because Cliff arrived wearing overalls and galoshes. And he was obviously an old man. When he told them he was there for the marathon, the professional runners asked if he had ever run in a marathon before.

"No," replied Cliff.

"How have you been training?" they asked.

"I have cattle on my farm. I have no horses, so I run around to move them along."

The runners laughed.

You see, every professional marathoner knew with certainty that it took about seven days to run this race, and that in order to compete, you would need to run 18 hours and sleep six hours. That's what the experts all said.

Cliff Young was clearly not up to their standards.

When the marathon started, the pros left Cliff behind in his galoshes. (Later he would run with more appropriate shoes.) He had a leisurely shuffling style of running that targeted him as an amateur.

Cliff had no training. He did not know what the world-class runners knew.

You probably guessed that Cliff won the race, but that is not what is astonishing.

Cliff Young cut nearly two days off the record time.

How?

Because of his lack of training, he didn't "know" that you had to sleep six hours.

Cliff got up three hours early and just kept on shuffling along in his galoshes while the pro runners slept. Cliff said he visualized rounding up sheep in a storm. He finished the race in just five days.

He beat everybody. He was a sensation in Australia.

Now world-class runners "know" it's possible to run with much less sleep. They know that they can conserve energy by adopting an easy shuffling jog. Now they have adapted to a new way of approaching long marathons.

We are like the pro runners. We act, not always according to the "real truth" but according to some conventional truth given to us by well-meaning or not-so-well-meaning "experts."

The experts have blind spots.
And so do you.

The *Nocebo* Effect

You've heard of the *Placebo Effect*, right? That effect where doctors give a person a drug to help with an ailment, but what the doctors actually give is an inactive sugar pill?

And then the patient feels better as if the pill were the real thing.

Somehow the mind and body reacts to the suggestion of an authority.

People rarely hear about it, but there is also something called the *Nocebo Effect*, coined in the early 1960s. Doctors can suggest something negative and the mind and body responds.

> In the 1970s, doctors diagnosed a man with end-stage liver cancer. They gave him a few months to live. He died and an autopsy revealed a tiny tumor that had not spread. The doctors' planted the image of death, and apparently the man died of that expectation.

> In a 2007 study, a suicidal man took pills believing he was taking an overdose of antidepressants. He nearly died until the researchers gave him intravenous fluids and explained that he had been given placebos. The symptoms rapidly disappeared.

> In a 2009 study, researchers gave placebos to patients who were told they were being given drugs with bad side effects. Participants experienced burning sensations, sleepiness, fatigue, vomiting, weakness, taste disturbances, tinnitus, and upper-respiratory-tract infections. The nocebo complaints were not random, but were specific to the type of drug they believed they were taking.

All of these examples point to one thing:

Self-fulfilling prophecies are real.

When other people give you negative pictures, or when you give them to yourself, the mind and body responds. They deliver the negative results you expect.

Beware of toxic people,
toxic doctors, and toxic thinking.

The story so far:

You have a mind. Your mind functions as a complex filter. It stores pictures of yourself and the world.

The pictures may not match reality, they may even be outright lies, but they are regarded by the mind as "True."

The mind has two mechanisms that work together to create blind spots to anything that you do not value, and that does not match the mind's stored pictures. The Reticular Activating System (RAS) controls sensation and attention to help you focus. And the Adaptive Unconscious (AU) regulates your perception, self-image, and behavior to resolve any conflicting pictures.

The good news is these mechanisms help you focus and maintain consistency in your sense of self and reality. The bad news is they blind you to anything contradicting your stored pictures, your definition of self and reality.

Why? Because their job is to maintain your *Reality*, meaning your stored pictures.

You don't get what you want in life;
you get what you picture.

When you learn to ride a bicycle as a child you learn a simple fact very quickly. If there is a rock in the road, you don't focus on it. If you do, you end up hitting the rock.

It doesn't matter that you *want* to avoid the rock. The harder you try to avoid the rock, the more you are drawn to it. To avoid the rock, rather than focusing on the rock you focus on the path *around* the rock.

When you drive a car, you also notice this phenomenon. When you think about changing lanes and you check the rearview mirror, you begin to drift into that lane. You go where your attention goes.

> I remember watching America's Funniest Home Videos. A buddy was videotaping his friend skiing down the slope. The skier was so focused on his friend holding the video camera that he ended up skiing right into him, even though he obviously was trying to avoid him.

You don't get what you want *in life;*
you get what you picture.

The mind naturally moves toward and manifests the pictures it holds, another aspect of the RAS and the AU.

> This is why in disaster training, airplane pilots do not practice *crashes*; they practice *recoveries*.

> This is why fatalistic people who are convinced nothing will go right in their life so often find that nothing does.

This is why no matter what kind of person you want to be, if you are convinced you are fated to be a particular kind of person, that is who you become.

You don't get what you *want* in life; you get what you *picture*.

> *If you are not happy with what you are getting in life, change your picture.*

This may not always be easy, but it can be done.

Of course, if you don't believe you can change the picture, then your current picture is fixed. In fact, many people want you to believe your life is fated to be something outside your control; that you must follow the picture they give to you of yourself. They may paint a fated version of "Reality" that mysteriously enriches them.

It's no surprise that the picture they give you is often at your expense and to their benefit. We explore examples of this kind of manipulation in *Money and Wealth: What You Should've Learned as a Teen, Book 2* and other books in this series.

The AU makes sure that you act like your self-image. It defines this acting as "realistic" or "sane." The AU acts like a thermostat. When you don't act like "Who I am" you develop anxiety until you either start acting like yourself again, or you change yourself (your self-image) to align with the new picture of yourself.

In other words, by changing your picture of yourself, you change your internal thermostat. You change the automatic regulator in your mind.

Remember, if you "know" that you are not good in math or writing, then if you do well on a math exam or writing exam, you will suffer anxiety because doing well is not "Who I am." Your AU will correct for the error of success and you will do poorly on the next exam.

The same is true not only with reading and writing, but also with exercise and sports, personal and professional skills, and any number of things.

Yes, there is a certain amount of innate ability involved. But if you assume in advance that you're limited, how do you know if the limitation is real?

Why do people who've been in prison for decades have such trouble adjusting to the outside world once they are released? Why will they commit a crime in order to be sent back to prison?

Because freedom conflicts with their deeply ingrained *picture* of being an inmate. Freedom equals anxiety.

That's why imagination is crucial to experience.

We attract ourselves to a state of consciousness once we can *see* ourselves in it. If we see and hold the picture inwardly, the AU works to motivate us to make the outer picture change.

The subconscious is like the autopilot on an airplane.

If the autopilot is programmed (the subconscious repository) to head due west, that's the direction the plane will fly.

The pilot (the conscious mind) can override the autopilot temporarily and fly the plane north by turning the wheel.

But when the pilot lets go, the autopilot (the adaptive unconscious) takes over and steers the plane back onto the pre-programmed course, due west.

If the pilot wants to stay on the new course, she must *first go in and change what's programmed so the autopilot adjusts to the new course.*

Then she has no problem letting go of the wheel.

> *Remember, every moment*
> *you move towards and become like*
> *whatever you put your attention on,*
> *including staying where you are.*

In Chapter 9, we will explore specific examples of what you can do to change pictures.

The 95% Certain Rule

As you can see, the mind creates blind spots whenever you claim to be 100% certain of anything. If there is any evidence that contradicts your 100% certainty, you will not see it.

> *Certain kinds of absolute conviction*
> *blind you to the Truth.*

But you can let go of these absolute convictions in order to test them. In other words, we find value in holding a kind of objectivity where deeply held beliefs (especially negative and limiting beliefs) are challenged and dissolved to form a more flexible and adaptive consciousness.

What can you do?

> Simply cultivate a bit of humility. Have a little bit of healthy self-doubt about everything you are certain is true.

> Say to yourself, "Yes, I believe that's 95% true; of course there is a chance I could come upon evidence or arguments that can change my mind."

Yes, some truths appear to be absolute. I could say to myself, "It is absolutely certain that I will not be able to jump to the moon two weeks from now."

But I have cultivated a habit of being suspicious of absolutes. So instead I say for the benefit of my subconscious, "It is highly unlikely that I will be able to jump to the moon two weeks from now."

> *Healthy humility about being certain*
> *entails little risk and helps keep your mind clear*
> *so you can stay flexible and see more clearly.*

Let's now focus on your self-image, and what influences it.

Chapter 8

Self-Talk and Self-Image

The Possible's slow fuse is lit
By the Imagination
Emily Dickinson

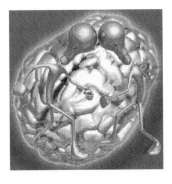

The subconscious repository functions somewhat like a computer. It accepts programming, lines of code, in the form of Self-Talk.

Self-Talk is what we say to ourselves *about* ourselves in our own mind. It's our Inner Dialogue.

Your Self-Talk programs your Subconscious
like a programmer programs a computer.

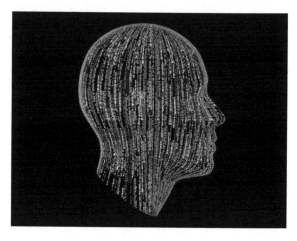

Self-Talk also includes those statements we accept from others as true, statements that we adopt as our own in our own thoughts.

> You've probably noticed how much your mind chatters about yourself and the world. For most of us, the mind is talking non-stop.
>
> That talk is not just what you say about yourself. It also includes talk from parents and teachers and colleagues and political pundits and advertising and... everyone whom we have consciously or subconsciously accepted as authorities.

If you were to monitor your Self-Talk for a day, you'd likely notice that, as with many people, your Self-Talk is mostly negative—angry, sarcastic, self-belittling, limiting,

can't-do, and down on yourself. It includes how you *feel* about yourself.

Your Self-Talk creates your Self-Image, the deep picture, which includes feelings, that is stored in your subconscious and filters your reality about yourself. Therefore, your Self-Image strongly influences How You Act in the World. And How You Act in the World reinforces your Self-Talk.

This is the Self-Talk Triangle that drives your sense of self and reality.

— Self-Talk creates Self-Image.

— Self-Image influences How I Act in the World.

— How I Act in the World reinforces Self-Talk.

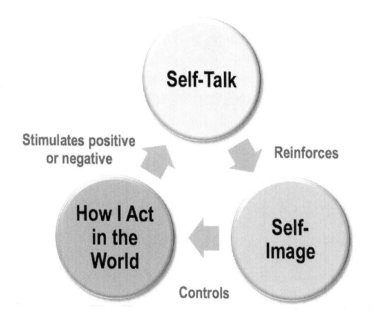

This Self-Talk Triangle operates mostly without people being aware of it. But when you are able to acquire enough detachment and begin observing the Self-Talk Triangle within yourself, especially your automatic Self-Talk, you can begin breaking the Self-Talk Triangle.

> *You become the driver of your Self-Talk,*
> *rather than your Self-Talk driving you.*

But this can happen only if you recognize several important things:

1. You are not a victim of anyone or anything.

2. You can begin recreating yourself and your reality.

3. You can continually enlarge your perception of Truth by overcoming your externally implanted and self-created blind spots.

4. There are plenty of people and institutions around you that do not want you to recognize any of this.

In a very real way, we are talking about your imagination, your primary creative picture-making and feeling-making faculty, your ability to create and feel a Vision about you and the world.

Look at your life and relationships.

Who and what is it around you that wants you to believe you are a victim?

That you should feel guilt or fear?

That you cannot help who or what you are?

That making your own way in the world is useless and pointless?

That you are helpless?

Who wants you to believe that you were born with a negative stamp on you?

Religious guilt?

Racial deprivation?

Some other thing that means you started out with a deficit that you cannot help? That you cannot overcome?

Who wants you to believe that you were born with limitations or grievances when compared to other babies born the same day?

Who wants you to believe that you are a victim?

> I have a friend named Ted who grew up with an older brother. His brother used to sing this song all the time:
>
> *Wrong Ted, wrong again, wrong all the time*
> *Every day, every week, wrong wrong wrong!*
>
> Can you imagine how this affected him?
>
> This song played in his head as an adult. He finally realized that this inner song affected how he thought of himself and his ability to function in the world.

So he changed the song. He changed his
Self-Talk:

*Right Ted, right again, right all the time
Every day, every week, right right right!*

Who gives you words and images to make you believe
that you cannot better yourself despite the way the world is?

Who uses guilt and fear and strong emotional energy to
"lock-in" negative imagery about you and the world?

Who tries to drive your behavior into thinking and
actions that steal your creative energy for an external cause?

Who wants you to believe that you can't change
yourself?

Who wants you to believe you can't change what is *True*
just by thinking differently about yourself?

*Remember:
If you don't use your imagination,
others will.*

Like little hamster wheels, thoughts within you run
constantly. They are running right now. Are they positive
or negative?

In the next 24 hours, try a little experiment. Pay
attention to your thoughts and ask yourself...

How much of my Self-Talk is negative?

Negative, sarcastic, devaluing, and objectifying self-talk
reinforces a negative self-image. A negative self-image

establishes subconscious patterns of behavior that can degrade how you perform in the real world.

Negative, sarcastic, belittling, devaluing Self-Talk creates a negative Self-Image and drives Actions that reinforce the negative picture.

Can't!

Why do you always...?

That's impossible...

Wrong!

You're not the type...

You're just not good at that...

That's not your strength...

Give it up!

See? You shouldn't have tried...

We can't do that!

They are the problem!

Ha, ha! That was foolish...

You may be surprised how many of those voices within are negative. But you *can* change and take charge of those voices. You can choose the voices that speak within you.

Let's look at how to do just that.

Chapter 9

Affirmations

Imagination is everything.
It is the preview of life's coming attractions.
Albert Einstein

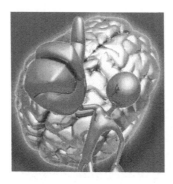

Despite its positive tone, this book doesn't have any final answers for you.

Answers often don't come from others. In many ways, we can't teach others. Sometimes others may *catch* something from us, but they often teach themselves.

Perhaps you might catch one or two pieces of truth in this little book. And that's really the point, isn't it?

> I know that my wife, and others, are always suggesting various traditional and non-traditional remedies for what ails me. I'm sure most of it works some of the time for some people.
>
> But it has to be the right remedy at the right time for the right person.

The same with advice.

There are no catch-alls—no sugared affirmations—that are guaranteed to work. But there are some things that perhaps you will discover for yourself.

> — I have a mind, but I am not my mind.

> — My mind is a good slave, but a poor master.

> — There are *hamster wheels* in my mind that can run me ragged, round and round with thoughts that can drag me down.

> — My mind's hamster wheels can drive me into melancholy, anger, and despair.

> — The hamster is my own *thinking and feeling,* my own inner dialogue. What I think, picture, and say about myself—how I feel, how I *should* feel, how I believe I am, how much of a loser I am—creates that reality for me.

> — What I think and talk about, in relation to others and the world, often creates that reality for me as well.

— My mind holds pictures about me and the world that eventually manifest the longer I hold those pictures in my mind.

— When I hold negative pictures about myself, I become those pictures.

— When I hold negative pictures about the world, the world reflects back those pictures.

— My mind operates automatically when I don't direct it; it will run off with those negative pictures, as if the default setting in the mind is *Negative*.

> *You become what you dwell on.*
> *You move toward what you picture.*

Remember, your thoughts are like lines of code in the computer program of your life.

The 15 Times Exercise

The way to break the Self-Talk Triangle is to reprogram your mind's autopilot. Take hold of your inner dialogue and work hard every day, every hour, every minute, to release the negative pictures and negative talk.

But not by resisting them.

The mind seems to work by the *Law of Reversed Effort*. The more you try to resist negative thoughts, the more you give them life. (Like focusing on the rock when riding a bicycle.)

The trick is *not* focusing on getting rid of those thoughts and pictures. The trick is *replacing* them with positive pictures. Focus on the positive.

Easily said.

One technique is the 15 Times Exercise. You take a positive affirmation and write it 15 times each day.

Many people write positive affirmations every day. But that in itself is not enough to change the mind. What seems to work more often for some people is the Change Formula, a kind of imaginative exercise:

IVF = C

Imagining Vividly *with* **Feeling** *results in* **Change** *(to the subconscious repository)*

You write it. You mentally say it. You vividly picture it, investing it with as much *emotional* feeling as possible. That combination gradually begins to change the pictures in the mind.

Words = Limited effectiveness

Words and Pictures = good effectiveness

Words, Pictures, and Feelings = great effectiveness

Here's an example...

> In January of 2013 I weighed about 258 pounds. I had a waist size of 40, and wore XXL shirts. I decided it was time to lose weight.

I started by writing 15 times every day:

"I love eating only proteins and vegetables, and watching my weight go down each week."

And as I wrote, I exercised my imagination.

I visualized eating steak, chicken, lamb, and fish with fresh salads and steamed vegetables. I erased potatoes, rice, wheat, pastas, corn, and sugars (carbohydrates, or carbs, and starches) from that picture.

I visualized looking at the scale and seeing my weight go down a pound at a time.

Then I put *feeling* into it. I *felt* the tightness of my pants loosen. I *felt* the healthy foods nourish my body. I *felt* the fat melt away.

Around this time, my wife took an extended sabbatical, planted a garden, and began cooking all my meals. She removed almost all carbohydrates from my diet.

She also did some research. She found that there are essential proteins, essential fats, and essential oils, *but no essential carbs.*

By September 2013, I weighed 228 pounds. I had lost 30 pounds.

I've enjoyed getting rid of my old clothes and fitting into new ones. My Levis have a waist size of 36, and my shirts are XL.

And I stayed with the diet long enough for my body to shift away from its built-in food habits. Now some carbs make me feel lousy, especially combinations of wheat and potatoes.

It's a new world.

Remember, the mind is a creature of habit. Left to itself, it will run negative programming automatically (unless you were raised in a profoundly positive family and with friends who actively reinforced a positive outlook on life).

The mind's habits will continue, you will experience those hamster wheels, *as long as you don't do something about it.*

You can see why other people might be interested in making sure you never get clued in to this fact:

You can control your own mind,
your own imagination,
your own reality.

Many people in life here, including scientists and politicians, may tell you that you can't take charge.

Don't buy into that. You can take charge by using imaginative exercises that vividly affirm the change with feeling.

It's difficult to break mind habits, to break the melancholy and despair, but it can be done.

One way is to moderate your intake of toxic thoughts, toxic environments, toxic people—

thoughts, environments, and people who tear you down. Especially family members like my friend Ted's brother in Chapter 8.

People who say, "You don't have the ability to live that dream."

People who say, "You are cold, heartless, weak, cowardly, stupid, and bad."

People who say, "The tests show you should try something else."

> *You're better than you think you are,*
> *and you can create a better self*
> *than you know.*

When writing a positive, powerful statement in the 15 Times Exercise, remember to write it in the present tense. Assume it's happening now. Assume it's already true.

Imagine it. Exercise it daily.

Don't write: I will write my affirmations every morning.

Write instead: I love writing my affirmations every morning.

Add some emotion to it. Feel it. Visualize it.

> *Imagine*
> *vividly*
> *with feeling.*

The subconscious repository loves emotion and pictures. It stores ideas more quickly when emotions and pictures attach to the ideas. It responds to imaginative exercises.

Being an End-Result Thinker

To overcome blind spots and achieve extraordinary goals, you must become an End-Result Thinker. Once you set a Goal, then your Reticular Activating System (RAS) lets through the information you need to achieve your goal.

Let me give you an example of that last principle. The RAS only lets through what you value or see as a threat. When you set a goal, you tell your RAS that you now value anything associated with achieving that goal.

This is why you:

> DO NOT WAIT FOR THE RESOURCES FIRST
> BEFORE SETTING OUT TO ACHIEVE A GOAL.

Sorry for yelling, but this point is crucial.

If you think in terms of having to have the money or resources first, you are doing it backwards.

You set the goal first,
then look for resources to achieve it.

Let your RAS do the work. Because once you set a goal, once you value it, everything that supports your goal will get through your filters.

> I once was asked to conduct a choir in front of thousands of people. I had never

conducted a choir before. I had six months to get a choir together and somehow get them ready for a performance.

Even though I had no experience, I agreed. I set the goal trusting that my RAS and AU would help me somehow.

A few days later, I walked through a used book store looking for a mystery novel. As I walked through the Music section, something caught my eye; something that I would have missed at any other time.

A book title jumped out at me: *How to Conduct a Choir.* I swear this is true. That book helped me greatly.

But I was not content to stop there. I told everyone I knew that I was going to conduct a choir for the first time and that I needed any help I could get. I opened up the RAS of my friends, so that if any of them came upon something, they'd let me know. (The power of networking.)

And someone did. A friend heard about a mutual friend who had once been a vocal coach. I contacted that person and got personal tutoring. She joined the choir, which also helped.

Don't wait until you have the resources before setting a goal. Stretch yourself. Set a stretch goal, even one that seems unrealistic, and see how life supports you. Here's an extreme example.

> I play piano. In my college days, I didn't have one. I couldn't afford to buy or rent one. For the longest time that stopped me from getting a piano. Why? Because I thought (held the picture) that I could only have a piano if I bought or rented one. I thought I needed the money first.
>
> Wrong!
>
> Once I was presented with the picture of being an End-Result Thinker, not thinking I needed the resources first, I gave it a shot.
>
> I began picturing having a piano and looking for a way of getting one that I didn't have to buy or rent. Once I set the goal, I soon had this thought:
>
> *Hey, you know there are probably people out there who have a piano and find it a burden. I could offer to store it for them.*
>
> Actually, I thought, there are probably people with *two* pianos who would *love* to have me take one off their hands. That way, they would probably let me keep it for years, since they already had one piano.
>
> So at my job as a 7-11 manager (putting myself through college), I began asking all

my regular customers who had known me for some time whether they had an extra piano that they would like to have someone store for them.

It took only *two weeks*. An older gentleman who lived nearby said his wife had two pianos and they had been thinking what to do with them since they needed only one.

I arrived that weekend with a friend and a truck. We walked into a very nice home. One piano was an older black upright Baldwin piano. The other was an even older, beautifully crafted Chickering spinet piano with a top that folded down turning it into a table. It was lovely.

We started heading toward the upright piano, and the man said, No, my wife likes the touch of that piano, please take the Chickering.

It was incredible! Beautiful appearance. Wonderful touch. Bell-like tone. I had that piano in my home for almost five years.

Even today, the piano in our home belongs to someone who has no room for it right now.

So you see, it wasn't a matter of Positive Thinking. It was more a matter of End-Result Thinking and applying imaginative exercises.

Thinking differently,
not harder.

It required no extra effort. Just a willingness to suspend disbelief and recognize that the possibilities of achieving a particular goal are much wider than we often believe. We just have to think from the End, As If.

> I *knew* there was a way to get a piano without buying or renting one.
>
> I set the *goal.* I saw it, I felt it, I acted as if it were a done deal.
>
> I got the piano within a couple of weeks.

Try it. Pick any instrument you've always wanted, for you or your child. You will be amazed.

Remember:
You create your life every day
by writing, picturing, and feeling
what it is right NOW.

Here are a few sample affirmations to get you started. And remember, there are people who run 10, 15, even 20 or more affirmations each day. They retire each affirmation as they manifest, and then add new ones.

> — I love exercising every day; I love feeling my sweat, my beating heart, and watching the scale show I'm losing weight.
>
> — I embrace challenges, and with each success I'm motivated to achieve even more successes.

78

— I'm a giving and loving person, opening my heart to all life, and feeling a golden glow constantly in my heart.

— I enjoy facing my fears, embracing courage, feeling fear melt each time I face it with courage.

— I love applying myself to my daily disciplines; I feel myself growing stronger and healthier as a writer/artist/coworker/manager/leader/etc.

— Success and good opportunities naturally gravitate towards me; among the lucky, I am the chosen one.

— I visualize and feel the end result with power and emotion, knowing it is true and present here and now.

Generally, the average affirmation takes about six weeks to take hold and manifest. Sometimes the time is shortened with intensive work, and prolonged with occasional or light work.

> So start right now. Write some affirmations on small index cards. (I use colored ones for fun.) Or download a pdf of an *Imagination Exercise Workbook* from the Resources page on my website at MarkAndreAlexander.com.

> Put your affirmations in a place you can write and review them every morning. Just take a minute or two on each. Remember to *feel them*. Build in powerful, positive emotions.

And watch your life begin to change.

30 Times for 30 Days

In 2012 I was explaining the 15 Times Exercise to some interns at the company I worked for. One of them told me that he knew from first-hand experience that writing affirmations worked.

> In college he needed to get a score of over 90% on a final exam in math in order to pass the course.
>
> A friend told him that if he wrote down the score he wanted 30 times every day for 30 days, he would pass the exam.
>
> So this intern wrote 30 times each day for 30 days, "My exam score is 95% and I have passed the course."
>
> *He got 93% and passed the course.*
> *Good enough to make him a believer.*

I think that no matter how many times each day, every day, you write your affirmations, there is something special about completing an affirmation around 1,000 times.

If you want to change more slowly, write 15 times each day for 10 weeks. If you want to change more quickly, write 30 times each day for 5 weeks.

And see what happens...

How to Be Realistic

I know some of you are thinking:

"Come on! You talk as if there are no limits. Of course there are limits. We're born with certain skills and talents and physical limitations. Not everything can change the way we want them to."

To some extent, you may be right. As I've said, I can imagine myself jumping to the moon, but that picture conflicts with certain natural laws.

People have differences and not all of them arise from the environment. Our genes do supply some limitations.

But consider the case of Rene Descartes, the famous philosopher who said, *"Cogito, Ergo Sum. I think; therefore, I am."*

(Did he really believe that he did *not* exist when he was *not* thinking? Perhaps he should have started with *I am; therefore, I think.*)

Descartes started from a point of supreme skepticism. He would lie in bed and think, What do I know to be true logically?

He worked out his philosophy of self and reality strictly on logical reasoning, not believing something was possible unless he could establish its logical basis.

Of course, there are some things that are true but cannot be reasoned logically using this method. Part of life does not submit to philosophical reasoning or scientific methods of proof.

(I know some things are true due to direct personal experience that I could never prove to anyone who has not had a similar experience. So do you.)

What I'm suggesting is that Descartes got it *exactly backwards.*

Because of the nature of mind and reality (and the historically limited views of what's possible, even among scientists), he should have started with assuming *everything* is possible.

Then he could work backwards adding on limitations to what is possibly true and logical once the evidence and arguments demonstrate the existence of limitations.

By starting where he did, Descartes could have created blind spots based on mere logic.

Don't consider what's written in this little book to mean you can do and be everything in this life. That perhaps *is* unrealistic. (Notice how I've implied the 95% Certain Rule.)

But do consider that you *have* accepted some limiting thoughts and feelings that you can now begin to remove and replace with non-limiting thoughts and feelings.

Writing affirmations and setting end-result goals *does* generate energy and motivates you to *work* more to achieve the goals you visualize.

You may not achieve them just sitting in the chair and wishing every day. You must work at it.

Look around at the successful people around you. They work *hard* every day.

Direct self-experimentation will show that you are capable of things you do not *currently* believe possible.

Try it.

What do you have to lose?

If I'm wrong, you have only lost some time in your life.

But if I'm right...

> *...think of the fresh and creative world*
> *that will open up to you.*

Chapter 10

Opening Windows of Opportunity

If you can dream it, you can do it.
Walt Disney

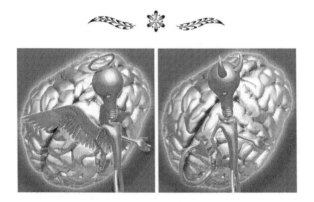

You may not know the story of Pygmalion.

Pygmalion was a gifted sculptor from Cyprus who one day found a large, flawless piece of ivory. He sculpted a beautiful woman and found it so lovely he became obsessed with the statue, thinking it his ideal woman.

He went to the temple of Aphrodite to plead
for a wife who would be as perfect as his
statue. When Aphrodite visited the studio of
the sculptor while he was away, she was
flattered to find that the image was of
herself.

Aphrodite brought the statue to life, and
when Pygmalion returned to his home, he
found his ideal had come alive.

In 1968 a study was done by two researchers, Rosenthal
and Jacobson that demonstrated what they called the
"Pygmalion Effect."

They told teachers that the researchers would test the
intelligence of children aged six to twelve years, all drawn
from the same school. They then randomly assigned
children to two groups.

Their teachers were told that the children in one group
were "high achievers" even though they were randomly
chosen. At the end of the school year, these children
showed significant test gains, despite the random allocation
to a group.

In short the researchers discovered that the teachers'
expectations manifested in the children.

*We can uncritically accept subconsciously pictures
other people hold of us.*

The subconscious repository stores our picture of
ourselves. When we are young, that picture is influenced
and reinforced by how other people picture us. Their
pictures of us affect how they talk and behave around us.

This leads to a couple of interesting ideas:

The Pygmalion Effect can work both ways.

First, you hold pictures of other people. Consider being very careful about the negative thoughts you hold of others, especially what you are sure is *true* about others.

Not only do you create blind spots about others in yourself that screen out anything that does not match your stored truths about them, you may also actually transfer your negative images to them in a way that they may adopt.

Second, be very careful about accepting as "true" any negative thoughts from others about you. Watch your own thoughts to screen out negative characterizations you may have accepted from others that may be holding you back, creating a negative, limiting picture of yourself.

> *Other people's opinions of you*
> *are no longer any of your business.*

We often carry multiple pictures of ourselves based on our current associations. In other words, different people may have given you different pictures of yourself, which can be triggered when you are with them. Or the pictures can be triggered in a situation similar to one you remember.

For example: Do you find that when you visit your parents, you become their child again, feeling how their image of you puts you in a box of behaviors that reinforce their picture of you?

Do you find that you are a different person—more confident, more capable, more articulate, wittier—around one group of people, and much less confident and capable and articulate and witty around another?

Do you find that when you return to old friends you haven't seen in years you fall into old picture-patterns that you had forgotten about?

Do you recall being known as a klutz or awkward in high school, and then after many years being a non-klutz away from those acquaintances, when you go back to them, you are suddenly that klutz again?

Have you ever been with someone, a spouse perhaps, who seems to undergo a personality change when around his or her parents or old friends?

Have you noticed how you change when you are with your church group, your drinking-poker buddies or shopping friends, your coworkers, your neighbors, your political group, your military pals?

Few of us maintain a single, consistent picture of ourselves as we move from peer group to peer group, or person to person.

However, over time, you can develop a strong, consistent self-image that does not change significantly when your environment changes.

Restrictive Motivation

Once you understand the picture-power of individuals, you can understand how manipulative people can "program" into you a picture of yourself designed to get in the way of you seeing the truth.

How?

By implanting in you *emotional* trigger points, which cause you to be reactive and therefore avoid what they don't want you to know.

First, here is an example where you can be programmed by a method called "Restrictive Motivation."

Restrictive motivation is simple to illustrate.

> Suppose as a child you had a stepmother who got violent whenever you were late. You're told to be home by 9:00 pm and you walk in at 9:15 and your stepmother yells at you and breaks things.
>
> The next time you're late, she yells and slaps you hard. The next time you're late after that she slaps you harder and locks you in the closet. The next time after that, she kicks you in the stomach.
>
> After a while, the *idea* of being late causes you emotional anxiety. You learn to flinch at the thought of being late.
>
> You're motivated to do everything possible to be home on time because you know what will happen when you're late.

Years later when your stepmother is no longer around, you will drive through red lights rather than be late for an appointment.

Even though the actual punishment is no longer present, your subconscious has taken in the *habit*, the *pattern*, the *imprint* of associating being late with punishment and pain.

But there is more...

Not only will you suffer this anxiety and flinch when you are late, you'll experience it when others are late as well.

You become a kind of controller of others when they are late. In order to relieve your own anxiety, you will go overboard faulting others for being late.

Why?

Because deep down a part of you knows that something bad will happen if anyone is late. You export your anxiety and try to control everyone around you in order to alleviate *your* anxiety.

Imagine having a boss or a friend who acts this way. Imagine that *you* act this way.

Now for a more directly manipulative example.

If I'm an accomplished political operative, I can program restrictive motivation in you. If I know that you avoid thinking deeply about hateful people, all I have to do is implant the picture that the people who are against my goals are hateful people.

You can recognize this kind of restrictive motivational programming whenever you experience a kind of knee-jerk, reactive emotional trigger. When your "buttons are being pushed."

It's a kind of reactive twitch that pushes you to avoid whatever is causing the twitch.

Try an experiment:

For the next couple of weeks, take note of anything that causes a knee-jerk negative reaction in you.

What kinds of things do you react to? And is it possible these reactions were *programmed* into you?

Kitchen Remodeling

One of the things that the Power of Positive Thinking crowd often fails to mention is that whenever you try to make a big change in your life, your life can sometimes enter a stage where it seems everything is falling apart.

When you want to take your airplane to a new altitude, put on your seatbelt because you may experience some turbulence on the way up.

Making a major change in yourself or your life is like kitchen remodeling.

You have your old kitchen. You're content with it out of sheer habit.

Then one day you visit a friend who has remodeled their kitchen. New granite counter tops, fresh matching appliances, new tile floor. You decide to remodel your kitchen.

Unfortunately, the transition to the new vision or goal is not immediate. *There is a dismantling period where your kitchen must be removed. You have a less than functional kitchen.*

You enter a kind of Dark Night of the Soul.

A less-functional or gutted kitchen means hard times. And there is always danger that if the new vision hasn't fully taken hold, you will hang on to the old kitchen rather than move forward into the new kitchen.

> *The new vision has to be stronger than the current picture to get you to act.*

This happens whenever you set a vision or goal and work to make it happen. The key again is that whatever goal you set, you must hold it strongly in mind.

> *If you hold the goal strongly in mind, if you daydream about it and feel it, you are more likely to achieve your goal.*

> *Your enthusiasm for the new vision carries you through the tough transition.*

You inspire yourself with it continually, and sustain the vision and energy through the rough times. Your old "anchor points," those fixed pictures that anchor your vision of reality, will get pulled up to make room for the new vision.

You hold the vision in order to have the energy to carry your goal through to completion.

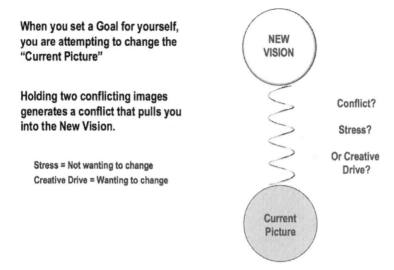

When you set a Goal for yourself, you are attempting to change the "Current Picture"

NEW VISION

Holding two conflicting images generates a conflict that pulls you into the New Vision.

Conflict?

Stress?

Or Creative Drive?

Stress = Not wanting to change
Creative Drive = Wanting to change

Current Picture

You want to become a chemical engineer. You are not one right now. But you know some chemical engineers, and their work fascinates you. You think you can be good at it and have fun with that kind of work.

So you hold a new vision of yourself that does not match your current picture. What do you do? You motivate yourself to go to school, do the work, get the degree, search for a job, go to interviews, accept a job offer, learn the job, grow in your new role. The vision manifests.

You have given up your old picture and adopted a new, more professional and experienced one.

The mind is easily distracted. Therefore, one has to work hard to keep the mind focused and disciplined. This is why people work with positive statements and affirmations.

Remember, to make a change, do the 15 Times Exercise.

I get a notepad, and every morning before I begin my day, I write a positive, changing statement 15 times. Currently, because my work has me sitting in front of a computer so much, I am writing, "I delight in physical activity and healthy exercise."

I know that "delight in" sounds funny, but there are several rules about the 15 Times Exercise that you must apply if it's going to work:

1) Write every day.

2) Use the first person present verb form, like "I am..."

3) Be positive. Say what you *are* doing, not what you are NOT wanting to do.

4) Use active, striking language.

5) *Visualize* and *feel* the statement as if it were a reality.

6) Remember the Change Formula: *Imagining Vividly with Feeling results in Change.*

When you do this imaginative exercise *every day* for months, once you make it a *habit,* you will notice changes take hold in your consciousness.

> *I recommend you start*
> *by doing imaginative exercises*
> *every day for 100 days.*

You will also notice that remodeling your consciousness is like remodeling your kitchen. When you hold a new vision, everything in you that contradicts that vision will come up. You will have to look at it and decide to either a) let it go, or b) take it back and not change.

Beware. *Something* will happen to try to interrupt your efforts. *Something* will try to get you to go back to your old habits. When it comes, *don't let it get to you.*

> *Hang in there doing your affirmations,*
> *hold to the new vision,*
> *until the new kitchen gets installed.*

After 30 years I had to give up caffeine in all forms. No coffee, tea, or soft drinks. Since I didn't want to be the kind of person anymore who was attached to caffeine, I began writing:

"I love being caffeine-free; I enjoy drinking water, juices, and healthy drinks."

When I gave up daily coffee, tea, and soft drinks, I held to that vision, even through the headaches and body changes and low energy days.

People tried to buy me those drinks. I hung in there. Now my body feels better than ever with more energy and more restful sleep.

You don't get what you want in life; you get what you picture.

Is your life more a comedy or a tragedy? Do you feel you have the ability to create your life, or does it seem like your life creates you?

One thing is clear.

*The mind is a good slave
but a poor master.*

Now you know that the mind tends to operate on a kind of habitual autopilot, generating thoughts and pictures of "the Truth," most of which we now recognize as being limited or limiting.

You now have some techniques to help you take charge of your mind and whip it into shape, rather than let it drive you every day.

What have you learned so far?

— We do not act according to the whole truth; we act according to "the Truth" as we believe it to be.

— When you lock onto a "Truth," it gets stored subconsciously and your mind begins working automatically to build blind spots to anything that contradicts that stored "Truth."

— Just because you cannot see it doesn't mean it's not there.

— You have all kinds of blind spots to the truth, to reality, right now, and there is a way to overcome those blind spots.

— High-performance thinkers recognize they have blind spots, and consequently strive to overcome them.

— To grow personally is not always a matter of working harder; it's often a matter of thinking differently, of thinking more effectively.

— Effective thinkers believe in their own ability to make things happen.

— Effective thinkers do not blame things outside of themselves; they feel their center of control inside themselves, not in external people or forces.

— The way we talk to ourselves can keep us fixed, or enable us to grow.

— You must become an End-Result Thinker to overcome blind spots. Once you set a goal, *then* your Reticular Activating System (RAS) and your Adaptive Unconscious (AU) lets through the information you need to achieve your goal. They also begin supplying energy to achieve the goal.

Remember:
Picture the End Result as if it were Now;
your imagination invents the way
to achieve your goal.

One note on setting goals: Be specific and clear about the actual end result.

Imagine a coach for a pro baseball team setting the goal for the team to get to the World Series.

Sounds good, right?

Wrong.

What happens when they *get* to the World Series? The goal is achieved and the creative energy and motivation goes out of the team.

The coach should set the goal for the team to *win* the World Series. Getting to the World Series is one picture. Winning the World Series is a completely different picture.

The AU regulates according to the picture given to it. Once the picture is achieved, the AU's work is complete.

This explains why you deflate after work or when you get to the weekend. If your goal is simply to get through the day or to the weekend, the energy goes out.

But when you set another goal, imagine something exciting to do, the energy comes back.

> If you doubt this, imagine after a day of work you are home, deflated. Then a great friend that you haven't seen for years calls, saying he or she is in town and wants to get together.
>
> Suddenly, you're energized, right?

> *Goals create energy and motivation.*
> *Imagination creates goals.*

Be sure to craft your goals precisely.

And then you can begin to sculpt yourself more consciously.

Secrets of Better Decision Making

In 2004, Annie Duke won the World Series of Poker in Las Vegas.

She did not start out as a poker player. In fact, she had been working towards a Ph.D. in Cognitive Psychology when, in 1991, a month before defending her dissertation, she got sick and moved back to her home in Montana.

Her brother was a poker player, and she soon found herself in a new kind of lab, studying how poker players learn and make decisions. She writes in her book *Thinking in Bets: Making Smarter Decisions When You Don't Have All the Facts*:

> "Over time, those world-class poker players taught me to understand what a bet really is: a decision about an uncertain future. The implications of treating decisions as bets made it possible for me to find learning opportunities in uncertain environments. Treating decisions as bets, I discovered, helped me avoid common decision traps, learn from results in a more rational way, and keep emotions out of the process as much as possible."

She illustrates what she means by "decision traps" by comparing success in life to success in chess and success in poker.

Success in chess is about making quality decisions.

Success in poker is about making quality decisions AND luck.

For Annie, *Life is Poker, not Chess.* And understanding that difference makes all the difference.

One decision trap is assuming that a *bad outcome* can always be traced back to a *bad decision.*

She gives an example of a controversial decision made at the end of Super Bowl XLIX in 2015 (the annual championship of the American National Football League).

> The Seattle Seahawks trailed by four points and had 26 seconds to score a touchdown. Everyone expected the coach, Pete Carroll, to call for a running play.
>
> Instead, the coach called for the quarterback to pass. The pass was intercepted and the New England Patriots won.
>
> Next day, the media headlines called it "The Worst Play-Call in Super Bowl History" and "A Coach's Terrible Super Bowl Mistake."
>
> There were a few dissenting voices, many of them pointing out the history of such interceptions in that situation was about 2%. But those voices were drowned out.
>
> What did the coach get wrong? Simple. The play didn't work.
>
> Think about the headlines if that play *did* work.
>
> "The Best Play-Call in Super Bowl History" and "A Coach's Terrible Super Bowl Mistake" and "A Coach's Incredible Super Bowl Win."

As Annie Duke points out, "Pete Carroll was a victim of our tendency to equate the quality of a decision *with the quality of its outcome*." (My italics.)

She explains that as she was learning how to play professional poker, other pro players would warn her to avoid the temptations of "resulting." Resulting means changing your strategy just because a few hands didn't turn out well in the short run.

And she points out that Pete Carroll understood this critical distinction when he said a few days later, "It was the worst *result* of a call ever… The call would have been a great one if we catch [*sic*] it. It would have been just fine, and nobody would have thought twice about it."

The media critics treated football like checkers. All the pieces are on the board and it is about making quality decisions.

In checkers you have all the facts.

But not in football. Like poker, winning is about quality decision, but it is also about *luck*. Sometimes it does not matter how good the decision is—sometimes luck works against good decisions.

In poker, as in football, and as in life,
you do not have all the facts.

In life, what makes a quality decision great has nothing to do with a great outcome. Sometimes great decisions still land us in not-so-great outcomes.

When creating your life, even when you are end-result oriented, beware of "resulting." Good strategies can have short-term failures while keeping you on the path to long-term success.

Stick with a winning strategy
and stand resilient against failures.

Chapter 11

Advanced Imagination: Creating from Soul

Imagination is the eye of the soul.
Joseph Joubert

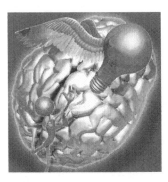

Up to now, we have focused on the mind as a tool to architect your life.

Creating from the mind.

But there is another way, one without much scientific research to back it up. But it may be worth your time to prove it to yourself.

Creating from Soul.

When you create from the mind, you can create only what the mind can imagine.

When you create from Soul, you can create what the mind cannot imagine.

> Many years ago I decided to create the perfect girlfriend using the visual mind techniques of positive thinking: visualizing her perfect looks and personality, picturing her sexual interests, affirming that she would come into my life, and applying what some call the Law of Attraction.
>
> And sure enough, I got her.
>
> *It took me two years to get out of it.*
>
> You see, the mind can imagine what it imagines, but you cannot account for everything with the mind. I got exactly what I visualized, but I also got a lot more that I didn't think about.

Creating from Soul is different. Rather than trying to create a specific picture of what I want, I aim for a "state of consciousness."

Here's an example of how my wife and I "manifested" our home.

Rather than picture our home, we pictured the state of consciousness we were aiming for. We wanted to be able to say, "Ah, we love our home without reservations."

It would be nice if we could get it for the exact price we were capable of paying. It would also be nice if it had space and light and water and room for a garden. Perhaps it would be nice to have workspaces separate from living spaces, and have it located somewhere on the Peninsula south of San Francisco.

But the target was that state of consciousness: "Ah, we love our home without reservations." And that included a turnkey home, one that was not a fixer-upper. But what would that *look* like? We did not know.

But we knew that we would not compromise on the vision, on the state of consciousness we targeted.

It was the late 1990s in Silicon Valley. People were bidding on homes beyond the asking price. Sometimes $150,000 or more beyond the asking price. Most bids were out of our predetermined price range, and those within our range came with homes that did not meet our needs.

Sometimes the house fit, but the space outside did not. Sometimes the space outside fit, but the house itself did not.

After we searched and passed on home after home for a few months, our real estate agent began to create a better a picture of what we wanted. He finally brought us to a home that was only three years old, built by an architect for himself.

The home had been on the market for several months, nobody had come to an open house the previous weekend, and we arrived with the seller already knocking down the price. The seller was a company that had moved the family for a job in another state and had taken on the house as part of the deal.

When we arrived, it did not look like much from the front: a driveway, a garage, a small front yard, and a wood fence with a gate and a small overhanging redwood tree. It was on a busy four-lane street. Not a good sign.

Our real estate agent opened the gate to a surprising inner front yard with a pond with small waterfall, geraniums, and other nice flowers and plants. The double front doors opened to an empty pristine home with an open-air atrium in the middle of the house with plants and a hot tub with another small waterfall.

The atrium was framed on all four sides lighting up the house, which was arranged around it. High ceilings, rooms open to each other, separate areas that could be workspaces (we both worked at home). And the backyard extended 60 feet beyond a large deck. Roses framed one side, and more flowering plants on the other.

We knew immediately this is what we had wanted without knowing it. No one had shown up for the open house the previous week, and it was clear the company wanted to be rid of this house that it had been holding for nine months.

So we offered $10,000 below what we were willing to pay, they came back with $10,000 above, we offered exactly what we were willing to pay, and they accepted.

Now as we close in on almost 20 years we can honestly say, "Ah, we love our home without reservations." For the exact price we were willing to pay. And new enough not to require any fixes.

I call this creating from Soul because something in this open technique allows a larger creative force to operate. I cannot say exactly what the mechanics are. All I can say is it has not failed me.

In late 2002 my consulting life, which involved working at home, underwent change, and I was ready for something new. But I had no idea what job I wanted. I just knew I had to make a change.

So rather than visualizing the job I wanted, I established the state of consciousness for that job.

I said to myself, "I want the kind of job that will challenge me in ways I could not imagine but I would find personally and professionally rewarding. I want work that rewarded me financially so that if my wife stopped working, I would be able to support us both. And I wanted work that allowed me to pursue the important personal activities that meant so much to me."

In July 2003 I consulted with a semiconductor company. I thought the work would last a couple weeks only. Instead, they liked my work so much, they kept me on. Eventually in early 2004 they made me a job offer and a chance at a new career.

Even though the job meant twice as many hours at half the pay (you have to pay your dues), I could not pass up the opportunity. I thought I could try it out for a year.

Three years later, I had a six-figure income.

Four years after that the company paid for my Master's degree in Organization and Management Development. I had acquired a whole new career in seven years.

My mind would never have imagined this kind of work or career. But I let go and trusted the process of creating from Soul and aiming for a state of consciousness rather than the specific limited imagery that my mind craved.

Somehow life found a way to fill it in.

Life can offer more
only when you trust it to deliver more.

Secrets of Failure

Successful high performance thinkers and creators understand the value of failure.

The innovation team at the Silicon Valley company that employed me had a strong motto:

Fail faster!

The great inventor, Thomas Edison, understood this idea. He ended his life with 2,332 patents worldwide. You may have forgotten some of his inventions:

— The incandescent light bulb

— The phonograph record

— The motion picture camera

— The carbon microphone, used in telephones until 1980

— A system for electric power distribution

— The fluoroscope

When asked about his failures in inventing a working light bulb, Edison reportedly answered, "I have not failed. I've just found 10,000 ways that did not work."

In other words, his failures were a form of success.

So how did Edison do it? How did he become one of the most prolific inventors in history? In a word, *attitude.*

Here are some of Thomas Edison's critical quotes:

> *Genius is one percent inspiration,*
> *ninety-nine percent perspiration.*

> *If we did all the things we are capable of doing,*
> *we would literally astound ourselves.*

> *Opportunity is missed by most people because*
> *it is dressed in overalls and looks like work.*

> *Many of life's failures are people who did not realize*
> *how close they were to success when they gave up.*

> *I find out what the world needs.*
> *Then, I go ahead and invent it.*

> *Hell, there are no rules here—*
> *we're trying to accomplish something.*

Edison had a rare quality—*resilience.*

Substances like rubber balls have resilience, the ability to spring back into its original shape.

Humans who are resilient have a strong capacity to recover quickly from difficulties, or in Edison's case, from failures.

Edison simply did not recognize failure. And this is how the innovators at my Silicon Valley company thought. *Fail faster* means recognizing that when you are innovating, creating something new that's never been done before, it is a *natural* fact that you have to move through a number of "failures" to get to success.

Failures are the norm for successful people.

> *They do not see failures as stumbling blocks.*
> *They see failures as stepping stones.*

"[Y]ou have no idea what you're capable of until you are tested. You have to allow yourself to be tested. If the circumstances of your life aren't already doing it for you, you have to push yourself and let others push you. That means that you are going to be uncomfortable and sometimes in pain, that you are sometimes going to be challenged, afraid, bone tired, and at your wits' end. You're going to want to give up if you're doing it right. But if you don't quit on yourself, you will find that you are capable of more than you ever thought you could be."

Kris Paronto, *The Ranger Way*

Chapter 12

Next Steps

*Creative people are curious, flexible, persistent
and independent with a tremendous spirit of
adventure and a love of play.*
Henri Matisse

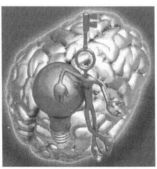

Marriage is a fascinating rite of passage.

Think about it. Before getting married, two people
walk around thinking of themselves as single, being
single, acting single. Then they go before a powerful

authority who declares, "Now you are married; go out and live it" and *prang!* They go out and live it.

They think of themselves as married, being married, acting married.

What really changes? Nothing but the *picture* they hold of themselves. The picture changes. Nothing else happens.

Often, people improve with the change in picture. Their hearts open wide, they become more giving, and they step into the best picture of themselves. Friends and acquaintances begin to see the newly married, no longer as mere separate individuals, but as a couple who embody unconditional love.

But marriage can go the other direction. Sometimes people go through profound personality changes when they marry. A whole new picture takes hold, because they "know" that this is how a "married person" is supposed to act.

> Men who seemed sweet and reasonable, who shared household burdens, suddenly demand that their new "wife" do all the cooking, cleaning, and laundry.

> Women suddenly expect their new "husband" to take on the natural role of handyman and protector.

Sometimes the change is more drastic and even violent.

What accounts for this change?

I've talked about how powerful our *picture* of the truth can affect our perception of Reality and the "Truth."

How the Subconscious Repository and Adaptive Unconscious works in setting and maintaining the *picture* of ourselves that we hold.

How the Pygmalion Effect works to give other people *pictures* of themselves, especially by people perceived as authorities.

A priest or public official is seen as a powerful authority to two people getting married. So powerful in fact that with a single declarative sentence, that authority can transform the deep-seated image two people have of themselves, to the point of an immediate personality change.

Think about that.

This is the primary function of *Rites of Passage.*

Rites of passage initiate the activation of a new picture a person holds of themselves. Before the rite of passage you are one kind of person. After the rite of passage you are another.

I grew up a math and science guy. On my SATs I scored high in Math and lower on Verbal.

In college I started out majoring in computer programming. After a couple years, I purchased a new Apple II+ computer, just when the industry was starting.

Then new personal computer magazines started appearing, and I saw one where the editors asked for submissions. I thought, *What do I have to lose?*

I wrote up a review of a computer security system. The editor wrote back and said, "We love your writing style. Why don't you expand this review into an article that compares security systems?"

Wham!

My picture of myself changed dramatically with that paragraph. Someone with authority said I was a writer. A good writer.

I wrote that article, they published it, and they paid me $200. I submitted my next article to a truck magazine about my friend's custom truck. They bought it!

Now I was a freelance writer.

I changed my major, and got a bachelor's degree in English.

Then when I took my Graduate Record Exam, guess what? The score in Math was *lower* than on the Verbal side. They reversed.

Early on, I saw myself as a math and science guy. Then I switched to a language and literature guy. I went on to work in Silicon Valley making a great income as a writer, and then developing managers in a tech company.

All because one authority said something powerfully good about me, which changed my picture.

The Wizard of Oz

Excellence coach Lou Tice, whose book *Smart Talk for Achieving Your Potential* is required reading, presents a wonderful way of looking at the movie *The Wizard of Oz*.

> Think about it. You have a girl with three characters, a Scarecrow who wants a brain, a Lion who wants courage, and a Tin Man who wants a heart. And the girl, Dorothy, wants to go home.
>
> So what do they do?
>
> They decide to go see the Wizard.
>
> Why?
>
> Because he is a powerful authority. He has the touch. He can give them what they need. He is transformative.
>
> So they go to the Wizard and quickly discover that he is just a man behind a curtain.
>
> But wait...
>
> It turns out that the ordinary man is more powerful than he appears. He is a real wizard. How does he do it?
>
> *The Tin Man wants a heart.*

The wizard tells the Tin Man that everyone who has a heart can hear it tick. So he gives him a clock to wear over where his heart would be and tells him in essence, "You have a heart. Go out and live it." *And he does*. Now the Tin Man can hear his "heart." He acts like he has one.

The Lion wants courage.

The wizard tells the Lion that everyone who has courage has a medal. So he gives the Lion a medal and tells him, "You now have courage. Go out and live it." *And he does.*

This is one reason why medals and other rites of passage are important in the military. Few people can go into a battle zone with the courage readymade. They must go through several initiatory rites of passage to adopt the *picture* of courage so they can be brave and capable and honorable under fire.

Finally, the wizard comes to the Scarecrow.

The Scarecrow wants a brain.

And what does the wizard give him?

A diploma.

(Think about that those of you who are about to graduate.)

The wizard gives the Scarecrow a diploma and tells him, "You now have intelligence. Go out and live it." *And he does.*

Think about it.

Someone wants to be a surgeon. They do not picture themselves as a surgeon although they study very hard.

They go to a graduation ceremony and before the ceremony they cannot cut into a person.

They accept a diploma, they are told that *now* they are a surgeon, go forth and act like it, and now they CAN cut into someone. What has really changed the morning before receiving the diploma and the evening after? Just the *picture* they have of themselves.

Remember:
You are now becoming
a powerful positive influence
on yourself and everyone around you.

Empowering and Destructive Wizards

You see, the Wizard of Oz was an *empowering wizard.* He gave people heart, courage, and brains.

But the world is also full of
destructive wizards.

People who steal a little bit of heart and courage and brains from others.

Who are the empowering or destructive wizards in your life?

Did you have a teacher who told you that you were not very good in something, thus stealing a little of your brains?

Did you have someone call you a coward and steal some of your courage?

Did you have a lover who called you cold and unfeeling, and steal a little bit of your heart?

What pictures did other people give to you that you bought into, simply because you perceived them as authorities?

But it goes further than that, doesn't it?

When were *you* unknowingly a destructive wizard?

When did you, out of anger, sarcasm, or embarrassment, take a little bit of heart, courage, and brains from someone who perceived *you* as an authority?

How many times has your own mind told you negative things about yourself?

How long have you been a destructive wizard to yourself?

If you are a parent, what kind of wizard are you to your children?

Do you consciously give them rites of passage?

Do you give them an image of the responsibilities and new opportunities available to a 12-year-old, when they are 11?

Do you use birthdays as rites of passage to initiate them into greater and greater pictures of themselves as they grow?

If you are a father, do you make sure your son goes through a rite of passage that helps change his picture and shift him into being a responsible man?

Has it ever occurred to you that the reason that there are so many boys in men's bodies is because these boys *never* went through a rite of passage to change their picture?

Girls have a natural biological event that ushers them into womanhood.

What do boys have?

They used to have fathers who took them hunting or camping, or did something that ritually ushered them into being a man. An adult male with adult male responsibilities.

How often these days is that particular rite of passage missed?

My father failed to provide me with a rite of passage into manhood. He was more interested in television and his own inner world.

I managed to change my own picture by:

1) getting a job at 16 and beginning to pay for my own clothes and hobbies; and

2) having my mother and stepfather tell me it's time to get my own place and pay my own bills when I turned 21.

My father was also a destructive wizard. Not out of malice, but because he was unhappy with himself, and so he took it out on others around him.

Once I discovered what he was, I spent time going through all of the destructive things he said about me.

I systematically changed all those pictures in me, letting them go, transforming them to positive pictures through contemplative techniques.

And you can do the same.

We are now near the end of this little book. So let's begin.

> Now is the time. The time for *you* to go through a rite of passage.
>
> Now is the time for you to become an Empowering Wizard.
>
> And I am absolutely serious about this.
>
> Ready?
>
> Okay.

By the authority granted to me...

by me...

a powerful, creative, Empowering Wizard:

I now declare that YOU are
a wonderful, creative, and Empowering Wizard,
who helps others grow into better persons.

Who now gives heart.
Who now gives courage.
Who now gives brains
to everyone you meet.

GO OUT, AND LIVE IT!

The *Creating Your Life* Checklist

The world is but a canvas to the imagination.
Henry David Thoreau

Take charge of your thoughts

___ Imagination is the tool with which you architect your life.

___ What you think, say, and feel creates your life.

___ Don't focus on the rocks in your life; aim for the ways around the rocks.

___ Let go of negative, angry, sarcastic, cynical, and self-negating thoughts.

___ Think of the end result without being concerned how you will get there.

___ Aim your arrows, relax, let go, and trust they will hit the target better than you can imagine.

___ Exercise choice: Choose your state of consciousness.

Inventory your potential blind spots

___ Pay attention to what makes you emotionally reactive and twitchy.

___ Think about those things you automatically reject as "crazy" or "insane," especially if you see these things in otherwise sane friends.

___ Note what others seem to see that you can't see: in religion, politics, business, science, and personal relationships.

Get in the habit of doing affirmations daily

___ Start right now: make your first affirmation "I love writing my affirmations every day."

___ Write every day, and apply imagination exercises.

___ Remember the Change Formula: *Imagining Vividly with Feeling results in Change.*

___ Try affirmations for 100 days: Give them a chance to work. If they don't, you have lost only time. If they do, you will have entered a completely new world.

Download a printable PDF of the *100-Day Imagination Exercise Workbook* at MarkAndreAlexander.Com.

___ Focus on the present and write what you are aiming for (not the rocks).

__ Trust that even if what you are trying to change grasps you harder, it will let go and you will be free.

Embrace change and flexibility

__ It's time to allow your dreams to enter into your life.

__ It's time to see yourself as worthy of your dreams.

__ Set goals that stretch yourself: Be realistic but challenge yourself.

__ Be the creator; no need anymore to allow others to create your life for their benefit.

__ Every day your goals become a reality.

__ Be an empowering wizard who builds up everyone you meet.

Your success and happiness lies in you.
Resolve to keep happy, and your joy and you shall form
an invincible host against difficulties.
Helen Keller

Go to MarkAndreAlexander.Com
to access a free 36-day course on *Creating Your Life*.

Subscribe to the "Creating Your Life" channel on YouTube.

Recommended Reading

Duke, Annie. (2018). *Thinking in Bets: Making Smarter Decisions When You Don't Have All the Facts.* Penguin Books: New York, NY.

Gladwell, Malcolm. (2008). *Outliers: The Story of Success.* Little Brown and Company: New York, NY

Paronto, Chris. (2017). *The Ranger Way.* Hachette Books: New York, NY.

Tice, Lou. (1995). *Smart talk for achieving your potential: 5 steps to get you from here to there.* Seattle: Pacific Institute Publishing.

Wilson, Timothy. (2004). *Strangers to Ourselves: Discovering the Adaptive Unconscious.* Harvard University Press: Cambridge.

For scientific research into the mind, behavior, and motivation, see the References listed in the Appendix.

Appendix

Scholarly Background

He who has imagination without learning
has wings but no feet.
Joseph Joubert

In 2010 researchers demonstrated the power of imagination. They knew that when people become habituated to eating certain foods, such as cheese, that people would eat less of them. They conducted five experiments against control groups having people imagine eating certain foods and then observing their subsequent consumption.

Their findings suggest "that habituation to a food item can occur even when its consumption is merely imagined" and that "mental representations alone can engender habituation to a stimulus" (Morewedge, Young, & Joachim, p. 1530). This research continues decades of studies correlating the pictures or visions that people hold or practice and their performance.

In 1994 Driskell, Copper, & Moran conducted a meta-analysis on the literature trying to determine the extent to which mental practice enhanced performance. The results indicated:

> ...that mental practice has a positive and significant effect on performance, and the effectiveness of mental practice was moderated by the type of task, the retention interval between practice and performance, and the length or duration of the mental practice intervention. (p. 481)

The history of research on performance reveals a heavy focus on peak performance in athletes. An article by R. J. Harmison (2006) cites research correlating psychological and behavioral skills and strategies with peak performance in athletes, "including (a) goal setting, (b) imagery, (c) competition and refocusing plans, (d) well-learned and automatic coping skills, (e) thought control strategies, (f) arousal management techniques, (g) facilitative interpretations of anxiety, and (h) attention control and refocusing skills" (p. 234).

The research that follows indicates that a conscious understanding of the functions of the reticular activating system and the adaptive unconscious can enhance these eight skills and strategies, particularly goal setting and imagery, and thereby contributes to peak performance in sports and areas beyond sports.

Reticular Activating System

> [I've] emphasized the importance of fixing, in your mind, a vivid picture of your goals. I said that once a specific goal is imprinted in your subconscious, an "alerting device" in your brain can then help you

find information you need to accomplish it. That unique device is the filtering device I just described: *the reticular activating system.* It's the most essential tool you have to lead you to success. (Tice, 1989, p. 58, italics in the original)

According to Siegel (2002), the reticular activating system (RAS) was identified in 1949 by Moruzzi and Magoun as the part of the brain that regulates levels of arousal, primarily the neural control of waking and sleeping (p 35). Siegel further notes that later research by Dell, Bounvallet, and their colleagues demonstrated how the RAS can be influenced by the cerebral cortex to inhibit arousal; for example, any incoming information that is perceived to lack value to conscious awareness (boring, meaningless, inconsequential) gets screened out (pp. 56-58).

Essentially, the RAS acts as a filtering mechanism, shutting down any distracting sensory input; what a person does not value, does not get through. Cognitive science researchers take into account the RAS when studying—and developing theories of—attention control, motivation, and task performance (Pribram & McGuinness, 1975; Kirby & Das, 1990; Stewart, 1996; Bernard, Mills, Swenson, & Walsh, 2005).

> The adaptive nature of the RAS operates mostly unconsciously; sensory input is screened out as the mind loses interest or devalues it. Often a person can be aware of the screening activity after the fact. When someone reads a novel and becomes immersed in that fictional world, the outside world begins to fade. Another person can talk to the reader and the reader does not hear that person. When a student finds a teacher boring, the student's

mind begins to wander and the teacher's voice fades from conscious awareness. Often a teacher has to call loudly on the student to attract notice.

Tice (1989) seems to be the first one to articulate how the filtering function of the RAS acts like an executive secretary, filtering out the thousands of sensory inputs happening in a given moment, "screening out the junk mail" and allowing you to focus on what's important, what's of value (p. 59). And like an executive secretary, the RAS allows you to focus on your goals. Tice provides many examples of how understanding the adaptive nature of the RAS can aid how one sets goals: "*The goal comes first, and then you see. You do not see first*" (p. 61, italics in original).

In other words, if you base goal setting on what you see now, your current resources, you limit the ability of the RAS to work in your favor. But when you set goals without knowing how you will acquire the resources to achieve those goals, the RAS opens up and lets through what is now valuable. According to Tice, you should not set goals only when you can see how to fulfill them (1995, pp. 137-140). Because of the nature of the RAS, you begin to see the resources once you set the goal. What you value gets through the executive secretary.

This automatic processing is apparently so much a part of people that behavioral goals can be activated unconsciously and can continue to operate unconsciously. Bargh, Gollwitzer, Lee-Chai, Barndollar, and Trotschel proposed this phenomenon and published research demonstrating how it can work in relatively simple environments (2001). The researchers concluded that since only so much conscious attention can be applied to the present moment, the unconscious activates unconscious goals so the conscious mind can "ponder the past or plan for the future" (p. 1025).

Ferguson and Bargh confirmed that setting goals triggers an automatic unconscious evaluation of goal-relevant objects as valuable, aligning behavior toward those objects as opposed to those that are evaluated as non-relevant (2004).

Adaptive Unconscious

If we are unhappy with our self-views, there are things we can do to change both our story and our adaptive unconscious. It is not easy. But little steps can lead to big changes, however, and all of us have the ability to act more like the person we want to be. (Wilson, 2002, p. 221)

There's more to what cognitive science calls the "adaptive unconscious" (AU). According to Wilson, cognitive and social psychology has pulled back the veil on the extent to which we can operate unconsciously, automatically processing our environment, generating automatic perceptual and behavioral responses, and often operating in ways quite different from the old psychoanalytical point of view of the unconscious (2002, pp. 4-5).

Wilson defines the adaptive unconscious as the "ability to size up our environments, disambiguate them, interpret them, and initiate behavior quickly" (p. 23). Our senses take in 11 million pieces of data in each moment, but we can only consciously process up to 40 pieces per second (p. 24). The remainder gets filtered out by the RAS, what Wilson and others call "selective attention" (p. 26).

But the AU in a fuller sense goes beyond mere filtering of information; abundant research shows that it also interprets information, acting both as a gatekeeper and a spin doctor (p. 31). Anderson points out how the subconscious is known for being a kind of repository for repeated behaviors, turning those behaviors into automatic actions, like driving a car (2005, p. 99). One can focus on others things and drive for minutes or miles forgetting about consciously driving the car.

Anderson discusses some of the dramatic demonstrations of such parallel processing that relieves the conscious mind of habitual behaviors, including one study showing how people could learn to read silently for comprehension while also writing oral dictation, and another demonstrating triple processing involving transcription typing (p. 100).

Furthermore, the AU generates feelings that can help us make wiser decisions. Wilson cites a series of studies involving gambling with different decks of cards, where some decks paid off well and others did not. As the gambling progressed, participants tended to place larger bets on the decks that paid better. They could not articulate why they did this, but based their actions on a "gut feeling" (p. 32-33). Essentially, these studies among others demonstrate how the AU "gathers information, interprets and evaluates it, and sets goals in motion, quickly and efficiently" (p. 35).

But the AU does not necessarily perform this executive role accurately. The AU tends to regulate perception and action in order to make us "feel good" (pp. 38-40). Whatever we unconsciously define as our comfort zone, whatever we are conditioned to perceive as our self-image and our picture of the way the world works, is regulated by the AU so that when we wander outside our comfort zone, the AU kicks in and aligns both our inner and outer world to our inner picture.

Tice—who explicitly bases his curriculum on the discoveries of cognitive science (The Pacific Institute, n.d., websource), including the work of Bandura, Beck, and Seligman, among others—likens this process to a thermostat, which automatically regulates the environmental temperature via heating and air conditioning in order to keep us within a comfortable range. Once we become aware of this automatic process, according to Tice, we can use proven techniques to influence it by changing or expanding our comfort zone, just like changing the setting or expanding the temperature range on a thermostat (1989, pp. 122-140).

Tice notes how when we lock on to something our mind naturally begins to lock out everything else. This action applies not only to sensory perceptions, but also to what we believe to be true about ourselves, about others, and about the nature of the world (1995, pp. 84-86). If we strongly believe something to be true, we "lock out" being able to see alternatives to that truth, or evidence contradicting that truth. Clarkson, Tormala, and Rucker have conducted extensive research showing how increased attitude certainty increases resistance to persuasion (2008).

Wilson cites research on how habitual thoughts and attitudes—about ourselves, other people, and the world— get stored in the unconscious, and how the AU begins to regulate our perceptions and behaviors according to those stored "pictures," even to the point of stereotyping other people and shaping our perception of them (pp. 29-30, 52-54).

Not only do these unconsciously held pictures influence our perception of others, the AU can regulate our actions in such a way as to *influence* how others perceive themselves and how they behave (Wilson, 2002, pp. 54-46). The classic "Pygmalion" study by Babad, Inbar, and Rosenthal demonstrated how teachers holding a biased perception of students influenced how they treated the students, affecting the students' actual academic performance (1982). This study revealed that people who hold strong pictures of others and are perceived as authorities to the others, could strongly influence how those others perceived themselves.

For example, a teacher who thinks a student is innately weak in mathematics can instill in that student an unconscious picture of inadequate mathematical performance, and then the student will behave (self-regulate) according to that picture.

Self-Efficacy and Goal Attainment

Unless people believe they can produce desired effects by their actions, they have little incentive to act. Efficacy belief, therefore, is a major basis of action. People guide their lives by their beliefs of personal efficacy. *Perceived self-efficacy refers to beliefs in one's capabilities to organize and execute the courses of action required to produce given attainments.* (Bandura, 1997, p. 3, italics in the original)

Bandura notes how self-efficacy beliefs play an important role in influencing the goals one sees as attainable, and consequently what goals one actually sets (1997, p. 136). His research demonstrates that people construct personal standards that guide, regulate, and motivate their behavior; that when people hold to these standards, they achieve a sense of self-satisfaction and self-worth; and that this "[s]elf-influence affects not only choices but the success with which chosen courses of action are executed" (p. 8). He cites research demonstrating how real-world skills can be overruled by self-doubt, while extraordinary accomplishments can result from applying those same skills when one has a resilient sense of self-efficacy (p. 37).

In other words, whatever the skills one may have, perceived self-efficacy contributes strongly to performance. Low self-efficacy affects thought processes, lowers motivation, and creates avoidance behavior to some tasks, while high self-efficacy increases sociocognitive functioning, influencing people to "approach difficult tasks as challenges to be mastered rather than as threats to be avoided" (p. 137).

Bandura's research also demonstrates that people who exercise control over their own consciousness, who regulate what they think, can increase their personal sense of well-being (p. 145). The aim is not to repress wrong thinking. He cites research by Wegner that demonstrates how efforts to suppress wrong thinking can actually increase the problem a person is trying to solve. Wegner shows that the better approach is for the person to become absorbed in positive trains of thought (p. 146).

Critics of Bandura's self-efficacy theory tend to apply their critiques in light of their own theories. For example, Biglan (1987) critiques self-efficacy theory from a behavior-analytic point of view. However, Bandura's research over the decades has proven so strong that he ranks as the fourth most-cited psychologist behind Skinner, Freud, and Piaget (Bandura, n.d., websource).

Collective Efficacy, Positive Psychology, and Mindfulness

"Cultural awareness, then, is understanding **states of mind**, your own and those of the people you meet" (Trompenaars & Hampden-Tuner, 1998, p. 201, bold in the original).

Self-efficacy is a natural starting point for strengthening collective efficacy in teams and communities (Fernández-Ballesteros, Díez-Nicolás, Caprara, Barbaranelli, & Bandura, 2002), and in the case of global companies today, cross-geographical and cross-cultural teams. Bandura also sees self-efficacy theory as a natural fit with positive psychology (2008). He argues that how people think about problems is key to solving personal, professional, communal, and global problems.

Peterson's Values in Action (VIA) Classification of Strengths—including creativity, persistence, social intelligence, fairness, self-regulation, and appreciation of beauty and excellence—provides specific virtues to focus on in building self-efficacy (2006, pp. 32-33).

Furthermore, the relatively recent emergence of mindfulness as a means of integrating brain research with inner awareness, and an understanding of the AU, is now enhancing humanistic psychology by helping with the development of what Ryback calls "the coherent brain leading to an awakened state" (2006, 489). "The integration of mindfulness with emerging brain research leads to the possibility of modifying brain structure through conscious awareness, thereby restoring self-determination to its proper role" (p. 474). Mindfulness also seems a natural fit with self-efficacy theory and positive psychology.

All of these combine with an understanding of the RAS and the AU to strongly suggest that a properly designed program—focused on developing self-efficacy and applying specific self-empowering tools and techniques that positively change behavior by changing how goals are set and what gets stored in the AU—will effectively increase the self-efficacy and change adaptability of individuals and teams.

Wilson argues that self-knowledge matters, and that we can better ourselves by becoming objective observers of our own behavior, trying to see ourselves through the eyes of other people, and learning about ourselves by assimilating the findings from psychological science (2009, p. 387).

References

Anderson, J. (2005). *Cognitive psychology and its implications*. (6th ed.). New York, NY: Worth Publishers.

Bandura, A. (1997). *Self-efficacy: The exercise of control.* New York: Freeman.

Bandura, A. (2008). An agentic perspective on positive psychology. In S. J. Lopez (Ed.), *Positive psychology: Exploring the best in people* (Vol. 1, pp. 167-196). Westport, CT: Greenwood Publishing Company.

Bandura, A. (n.d.). *Wikipedia*. Retrieved 10 April 2011, from http://en.wikipedia.org/wiki/Albert_Bandura

Babad, E. Y., Inbar, J., & Rosenthal, R. (1982). Pygmalion, Galatea, and the Golem: Investigations of biased and unbiased teachers. *Journal of Educational Psychology, 74*(4), 459-474. doi:10.1037/0022-0663.74.4.459

Bargh, J. A., Gollwitzer, P. M., Lee-Chai, A., Barndollar, K., & Trotschel, R. (2001). The automated will: Nonconscious activation and pursuit of behavioral goals. *Journal of Personality and Social Psychology, 81*(6), 1014-1027. doi:10.1037/0022-3514.81.6.1014

Bernard, L. C., Mills, M., Swenson, L., & Walsh, P. R. (2005). An Evolutionary Theory of Human Motivation. *Genetic, Social, and General Psychology Monographs, 131*(2), 129-184. doi:10.3200/MONO.131.2.129-184

Biglan, A. (1987). A behavior-analytic critique of Bandura's self-efficacy theory. *The Behavior Analyst, 10*(1), 1-15.

Clarkson, J. J., Tormala, Z. L., & Rucker, D. D. (2008). A new look at the consequences of attitude certainty: The amplification hypothesis. *Journal of Personality and Social Psychology, 95*(4), 810-825. doi:10.1037/a0013192

Driskell, J., Copper, C., & Moran, A. (1994). Does mental practice enhance performance? *Journal of Applied Psychology, 79*(4), 481-492. doi:10.1037/0021-9010.79.4.481

Ferguson. M. J., & Bargh. J. A. (2004). Liking is for doing: The effects of goal pursuit on automatic evaluation. *Journal of Personality and Social Psychology, 87*(5), 557–572. doi:10.1037/0022-3514.87.5.557

Fernández-Ballesteros, R., Díez-Nicolás, J., Caprara, G. V., Barbaranelli, C., & Bandura, A. (2002). Determinants and structural relation of personal efficacy to collective efficacy. *Applied Psychology: An International Review, 51*, 107-125. doi:10.1111/1464-0597.00081

Harmison, R. J. (2006). Peak performance in sport: Identifying performance states and developing athletes' psychological skills. *Professional Psychology: Research and Practice, 37*(3), 233-243. doi:10.1037/0735-702.37.3.233

Kihlstrom, J. F. (2004). Is your unconscious smarter than you are? Review of: Strangers to ourselves: Discovering the adaptive unconscious. *PsycCRITIQUES, 49*(14). doi:10.1037/04095S

Kirby, J. R., & Das, J. P. (1990). A cognitive approach to intelligence: Attention, coding and planning. *Canadian Psychology 31*(4), 320-333. doi:10.1037/h0078948

Morewedge, C., Young, E. H., & Vosgerau, J. (2010, December 10). Thought for food: Imagined consumption reduces actual consumption. *Science, 330,* 1530-1533.

The Pacific Institute: A curriculum based on the foundations of modern cognitive science. (n.d.). Retrieved 3 April 2011, from http://www.thepacificinstitute.us/v2/files/pdfs/Curriculum Foundations.pdf

Peterson, C. (2006). The values in action (VIA) classification of strengths. In Csikszentmihalyi, M, & Csikszentmihalyi, S. C., *A life worth living: Contributions to positive psychology* (29-48). New York: Oxford University Press.

Pribram, K. H., & McGuinness, D. (1975). Arousal, activation, and effort in the control of attention. *Psychological Review, 82*(2), 116-149. doi:10.1037/h0076780

Ryback, D. (2006). Self-determination and the neurology of mindfulness. *Journal of humanistic psychology, 46*(4), 474-493. doi:10.1177/0022167806290214

Siegel, J. (2002). *The neural control of sleep & waking.* New York, NY: Springer.

Stewart, G. L. (1996). Reward structure as a moderator of the relationship between extreme extraversion and sales performance. *Journal of Applied Psychology, 81*(6), 619-627. doi:10.1037/0021-9010.81.6.619

Tice, L., & Steinberg A. (1989). *A better world, a better you: The proven Lou Tice "Investment in Excellence" program.* Englewood Cliffs, NJ: Prentice Hall.

Tice, L. (1995). *Smart talk for achieving your potential: 5 steps to get you from here to there.* Seattle: Pacific Institute Publishing.

Trompenaars, F. & Hampden-Turner, H. (1998). *Riding the waves of culture: Understanding diversity in global business.* New York: McGraw-Hill.

Wilson, T. D. (2002). *Strangers to ourselves: Discovering the adaptive unconscious.* Cambridge, MA: Harvard University Press.

Wilson, T. D. (2009). Know thyself. *Perspectives on psychological science, 4*(4), 384-389. doi:10.1111/j.1745-6924.2009.01143.x

"Helped me to decide to sell my house and buy another without a mortgage…"
— Diane Matlack

"Five Stars. Insightful!! Inspiring!!! This book is the economics class you didn't think you wanted… I was not expecting a succinct explanation of the economics we live with… My expectations were exceeded on all levels."
— Carl L. Chase

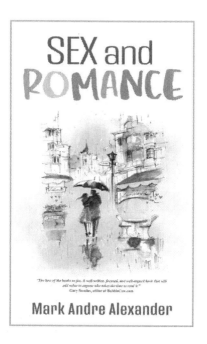

"The best of the books so far. A well-written, focused, and well-argued book that will add value to anyone who takes the time to read it."
— Gary Smailes, editor at BubbleCow.com.

"I was blown away. Although it's a fairly short read, Mr. Alexander has packed a huge amount of valuable and perceptive information for readers...Parents, teachers, counselors, clergymen, and basically anyone working and counseling teens and tweens will find this book an invaluable resource...filled with insightful quotes, common sense advice, and delightful prose."
— Susan Elizabeth Barton - eBook Review Gal

"Mozart's joy is made of serenity, and a phrase of his music is like a calm thought; his simplicity is merely purity. It is a crystalline thing in which all the emotions play a role, but as if already celestially transposed."
— André Gide, Nobel Prize-winning French author

"Mozart makes you believe in God because it cannot be by chance that such a phenomenon arrives into this world and leaves such an unbounded number of unparalleled masterpieces."
— Georg Solti, Hungarian conductor

"It is thanks to Mozart that I have devoted my life to music...Mozart is the highest, the culminating point that beauty has attained in the sphere of music. Mozart is the musical Christ."
— Piotr Tchaikovsky, Russian composer

About the Author

Mark Andre Alexander has a B.A. in English and an M.A. in Organization and Management Development. He works in Silicon Valley helping people take their next step. He has delivered training to engineering managers from around the world on High Performance Thinking.

He's a happy soul, a composer and musician, and likes to make people laugh.

Occasionally he publishes articles and books. He's married to a woman who improves him just by being present, and he believes everyone is on a journey to learn how to give and receive divine love.

Go to **MarkAndreAlexander.Com** to access a free 36-day course on *Creating Your Life*.

Subscribe to the "Creating Your Life" channel on YouTube.

THE SCHOOL OF
PYTHAGORAS™

*Whatever you hold in you mind is bound
to come into existence sooner or later.
The idea is the thing itself.*
Paul Twitchell

Made in the USA
San Bernardino, CA
28 May 2018